THE

THREE MESSAGES

OF

REVELATION XIV, 6-12,

PARTICULARLY THE

THIRD ANGEL'S MESSAGE,

AND

TWO-HORNED BEAST.

BY ELD. J. N. ANDREWS.

FIFTH EDITION, REVISED.

REVIEW AND HERALD PUBLISHING CO.:

BATTLE CREEK, MICH.; CHICAGO, ILL.;

TORONTO, ONT.; ATLANTA, GA.

1892.

2002 03 04 05 06 • 5 4 3 2 1

This book played a formative role in the development
of Christian thought and the publisher feels
that this book, with its candor and depth, still holds
significance for the church today.

Facsimile Reproduction

Copyright © 1998 TEACH Services, Inc.
ISBN 1-57258-125-5

Library of Congress Catalog Card No. 97-80511

Published by

TEACH Services, Inc.
www.tsibooks.com

PREFACE.

THE Bible is full of references to the second advent of the Saviour and the events of the great day of God. It represents that day as the great day of his wrath; as the time when destruction from the Almighty shall come upon the wicked, and when the land shall be made desolate, and the sinners thereof destroyed out of it. The language of the inspired writers expresses in the most vivid manner the awful and terrific scenes of that day in which God arises from his place to punish the inhabitants of the earth.

Shall mankind have no warning when this destruction is about to burst upon them? Shall there be no token of coming wrath to arrest the guilty in their downward career? Shall irretrievable ruin swallow up a sinful world, and God give them no intimation of its approach?

Such was not the case with the antediluvian world, nor has it ever been the manner of the just Judge of all the earth to visit mankind in judgment without giving them warning of the coming vengeance. The attentive reader of the prophets will find ample testimony in proof of this statement. The judgments of God upon Jerusalem, Samaria, Tyre, Nineveh, and Babylon, are striking illustrations of this fact. Shall we conclude that the last and most dreadful judgment of God shall come upon our earth without previous warning to its inhabitants?

The people of God at the commencement of the great day of wrath will be translated into his everlasting kingdom. That is, they will be clothed upon with immortality, and will never taste of death. What will prepare the saints of the last generation for such a distinguished honor? Will they be found at their Lord's return in a state of confusion and anarchy? Will this be their condition when their returning Lord shall take them in a body unto himself?

As the people of God, one by one, have fallen victims to the power of death, and individual work of preparation has been all that was requisite; but when the time comes that all the saints of God who are alive shall in one body be taken into glory, surely something further than an individual work is necessary. By what means shall the saints of God be gathered in one people and prepared for translation? What mighty truths has God in reserve for the last generation, with which to accomplish this great work? In answer to these questions, we cite the fourteenth chapter of Revelation.

The design of the three great proclamations of this chapter, is, first, to give warning of coming judgment; secondly, to set the people of God upon their watch-tower; thirdly, to gather in one body the scattered saints; and, fourthly, to restore the commandments of God to his people, and to prepare them for deliverance in the time of trouble, and for translation into his kingdom.

Such is the work presented in Rev. 14. It gives the world warning, and leaves them without excuse; it lights up the pathway of the saints; and yet, with its trial of patience, it shakes off the heartless, and gives the men of the world, notwithstanding its warning, a chance to lull themselves into security, when the wrath of God hangs over their heads.

Shall not these great truths arrest attention? Shall it be with us as with the antediluvians, who, warned of the coming destruction, nevertheless knew not until it came and took them all away? When the Son of man cometh, who of us shall be able to say, "Lo, this is our God, we have waited for him, and he will save us"?

J. N. A.

Battle Creek, Mich., Jan., 1877.

CONTENTS.

CHAPTER I.

TIME WHEN THE PROCLAMATIONS OF REV. 14 ARE MADE.

CHAPTER II.

THE PROCLAMATION OF THE FIRST ANGEL.

CHAPTER III.

THE PROCLAMATION OF THE SECOND ANGEL.

CHAPTER VIII.

THE PENALTY THREATENED BY THE THIRD ANGEL.

CHAPTER IX.

CHRONOLOGY OF THE THIRD ANGEL.

THREE ANGELS OF REV. 14:6-12.

CHAPTER I.

TIME WHEN THE PROCLAMATIONS OF REV. 14 ARE MADE.

Importance of the Subject—Different Views of this Prophecy—
These Proclamations not applicable to the Future Age—Nor
can they belong to Past Ages—The Messages addressed to the
Last Generation—Argument from 2 Thess. 2—From Dan. 12
—From the Signs—From the Parable of the Supper—From
Nahum 2—From the Destruction of Babylon—From the Work
of the Two-Horned Beast—Nature of These Proclamations.

WHOEVER will read attentively the proclamations embraced in the fourteenth chapter of Revelation, cannot fail to notice their vast importance.
At whatever period in the history of the church
these proclamations are made, from their very
nature they must constitute the great theme of
interest for that generation. Whenever the angels of this chapter are commissioned by God to
announce to the nations of the earth that the
hour of his Judgment is come, or to proclaim the
fall of Babylon, or to utter against the worshipers
of the beast the most dreadful threatening which
the Bible contains, no man can disregard their
work, or treat their warnings as non-essential, ex-

cept at the peril of his soul. If it were merely possible that these warnings were addressed to ourselves, it would become us to examine this subject with serious attention ; but if this point can be proved by decisive testimony, it is certain that we cannot too carefully attend to the warnings here uttered.

It was but a few years ago that all advent believers were united in applying this prophecy to the present generation ; but in the period of trial that has followed their disappointment, many of them have, to a great extent, lost sight of their original faith. A considerable number now contend that these angels are to utter their voices of warning in the future age ; that is, in a period subsequent to the second advent. Another class attempt to show that they had their fulfillment many ages in the past, the first angel beginning in the days of the apostles, the second in the time of Luther, and the third at a period somewhat later.

As proof that these angels belong to the future age, the fact is adduced that John saw them flying through the midst of heaven immediately after having seen the Lamb stand upon Mount Zion with the 144,000. As the latter event is future, it is concluded by them that the angels of this prophecy must be future also. If it were a fact that the events predicted in the book of Revelation were there given in consecutive order, there would be some force to this argument. But it is evident that that book is made up of many distinct views, usually introduced by the expression, "And I saw," or something of that kind, as in Rev. 14 : 6. The series of events which begins in chap. 12, with the dragon, evidently extends through the work of the beasts in chap. 13, and ends with a view of the remnant in their glorified state upon Mount Zion. Rev. 14 : 1–5. Then begins a new series of events with the angel of chap. 14 : 6.

The following reasons forbid the application of this prophecy to the future age :—

1. This view would make the angel with the everlasting gospel to every nation, kindred, and tongue, an angel from heaven with another gospel (Gal. 1 : 8); for the apostolic commission extended only to the harvest, which is the end of the world. Matt. 28 : 19, 20 ; 24 : 14 ; 13 : 24–30, 36–43. Paul participated in this commission (1 Tim. 1 : 11), and he thus declares its import : that God "*now* commandeth all men everywhere to repent; because he hath appointed a day in the which he will judge the world in righteousness." Acts 17 : 30, 31. The apostolic commission extended only to the end,—the day in which God shall judge the world by Jesus Christ. A gospel preached in that day would be another gospel than that preached by Paul, and one that has no Saviour in it. This would indeed show that the angel of Rev. 14 : 6, 7 was the very being on whom rests the curse of Paul in Gal. 1 : 8.

2. The second angel announces the fall of Babylon. Rev. 14 : 8. After this proclamation, a voice is heard from heaven, saying, " Come out of her, my people." Rev. 18 : 1–4. That the absurdity of placing this transaction after the second advent may be seen, please read 1 Thess. 4 : 16, 17. It is there plainly stated that at the coming of Christ, his people shall all be caught up to meet him in the air, and thenceforward be forever with the Lord. Will the Lord take his people to Bab-

ylon when he comes ?—Never.   He says, "I go
to prepare a place for you.   And if I go and prepare a place for you, I will come again, and receive
you unto myself ; that where I am, there ye may
be also."   John 14 : 2, 3.   Then the Lord will
not have occasion to call his people out of Babylon
after the second advent ; for from that time onward they are to be forever with him.

3. Let us now see whether the Third Angel's
Message can be applied to the future age with
any propriety.   Those who will compare Rev.
14 : 9–12 and 13 : 11–17, will see at once that the
warning voice of the third angel relates to the
fearful scene when the two-horned beast is to act
its part in oppressing the saints of the Lord.
But if the third angel's proclamation relates to
the period which follows the second advent, then
the work of the two-horned beast must also
transpire in the future age.   And what a scene
must the future reign of the saints present, if
Rev. 13 : 11–17 is to be fulfilled in that time !
But by turning to Rev. 20 : 4–6, it will be seen
that the period for the triumph of the beast and
his image, and for the reception of his mark, precedes the thousand years' reign of the saints.   And
when the reign of the saints commences, the triumph of the beast is past.

The beast doubtless represents the papal power.
Rev. 13 : 1–10; Dan. 7 : 8, 20, 21, 25, 26.   But
by turning to 2 Thess. 2, we learn that the papacy
is to be destroyed by the brightness of Christ's
coming.   Further, we learn from Rev. 19 : 19–21
that the final overthrow of the beast and the false
prophet, or the two-horned beast, takes place in
the battle of the great day of God Almighty, in
immediate connection with the second advent.

By these plain testimonies we establish the fact that the beast will be destroyed at the second advent. Therefore we ask, What danger will there be that men will worship the beast at a time when there will be none for them to worship? God will never send an angel to warn men against the worship of the beast when the beast does not exist.

The language of verse 12, "Here is the *patience* of the saints," is sufficient of itself to overthrow the application of these messages to the future age. The following scriptures clearly teach that the patience of the saints refers to the present time, and not to the period of their future glorious reward: "Ye have need of patience, that, after ye have done the will of God ye might receive the promise." Heb. 10:36. "In your patience possess ye your souls." Luke 21:19. ' Be patient, therefore, brethren, unto the coming of the Lord." James 5:7. Will the saints have need of patience in the kingdom of God? Will they have to possess their souls in patience after they have received the promise, even life everlasting? 1 John 2:25. It is tribulation that worketh patience. Rom. 5:3 James 1:2, 3. Are the saints in tribulation after they are made immortal and crowned with everlasting joy?—No, never. Isa. 25:8. 9; 35:10; Rev. 7:13–17. But the saints are in their patience when the Third Angel's Message 's given, hence that message does not belong to the future age.

But verse 12 concludes thus: "Here are they that keep the commandments of God and the faith of Jesus." It is evident that this refers to the period when the remnant are keeping the commandments of God while exposed to the wrath of the dragon (Rev 12:17), and that it does not refer to the period when the commandment-keepers shall have entered in through the gates into the holy city (Rev. 22:14); and that it refers to the period when the saints are living by faith (Heb. 10: 38, 39), and not to the period when they shall have received the *end* of their faith, the salvation of their souls. 1 Pet. 1: 9.

But verse 13, which pronounces a blessing on the dead which die in the Lord *from henceforth*, that is, from a point of time as late, at least, as the Third Angel's Message, presents a testimony which cannot be evaded. It demonstrates that this part of John's vision relates to a period prior to the first resurrection; for the saints cannot die after being made immortal. 1 Cor. 15:51–56. Our Lord testifies that they can die no more, but are equal unto the angels, and are the children of God, being the children of the resurrection. Luke 20: 36. If any are still disposed to locate these angels' messages in the day of God itself, let them carefully read the following scriptures: Matt. 24: 37–39; Luke 17: 26–30; Gen. 7:21, 22; Luke 21:35; Ps. 2:6–9; Rev. 2: 26, 27; 19: 11–21; 22: 11, 12; 2 Thess. 1: 6–10.

The next inquiry relates to the past. Have not these messages met their fulfillment in the history of the church in past ages?—We think not. Our reasons for this conclusion are, in part, the following:—

1. No proclamation of the hour of God's Judgment come, has ever been made in any past age.

2. If such a proclamation had been made many centuries in the past, as some contend, it would have been a false one.

3. The prophecies on which such a proclama-

tion to men in a state of probation must be based, were closed up and sealed to the time of the end.

4. The Scriptures plainly locate the message of warning respecting the Judgment in a brief space immediately preceding the advent of our Lord, thus directly contradicting the view that locates these messages in past ages.

We now offer proof in support of the foregoing propositions. If they are sustained, they establish the fact that the present generation is that one to which the angels' messages are addressed. We earnestly invite all who wish to find the truth, to weigh this part of the argument with special care.

1. Has the proclamation of the hour of God's Judgment come, been made in any past age? If such a proclamation has never been made in past centuries, there is an end to controversy on this part of the subject. No person has ever been able to show any such proclamation in the past. The apostles did not make such a proclamation; on the contrary, they plainly inform us that the day of the Lord was not then at hand. Martin Luther did not make this proclamation; for he thought the Judgment about three hundred years in the future. And finally, the history of the church presents no such proclamation in the past. Had the first angel preached to every nation, and kindred, and tongue, and people, that the hour of God's Judgment had come, the publicity of such a proclamation would be a sufficient guaranty that the history of the world would contain some record of the fact. Its total silence respecting such a proclamation is ample proof that it was never made, and should put to silence those who make such an affirmation.

2. We are on firm ground, also, when we say that had such a proclamation been made to the world in ages past, it would have been false. Four reasons sustain this statement: (1.) There is no part of the Bible on which such a message, centuries in the past, could have been based; hence, had such a proclamation been made, it would have been without scripture foundation, and consequently not from Heaven; (2.) It would have been in direct opposition to those scriptures which locate the Judgment, and the warning re-respecting its approach, in the period of the last generation. (The scriptures which sustain these two reasons we shall presently cite.); (3.) The history of the world amply evinces that the hour of God's Judgment had not come ages in the past; (4.) Nor would it be true of past ages, if limited to Babylon; for Rev. 18: 8–10 clearly shows that the hour of Babylon's Judgment is yet in the future. It is certain, therefore, that the angel with the proclamation respecting the hour of God's Judgment has not given it at a time when it would be not only destitute of scriptural support, but would absolutely contradict their plain testimony.

3. The prophecies which give us the time of the Judgment, and which present the succession of events leading down to that great crisis, were closed up and sealed till the time of the end. We refer particularly to the prophecies of Daniel. See Dan. 8: 17, 26; 12: 4, 9. Hence it is evident that God preserves the warning for that genera-tion which alone needs it. Noah's warning re-specting the flood was alone applicable to those who should witness it; thus also the warning re-specting the Judgment is alone applicable to that generation which lives in the last days,

4. The Bible locates these messages in the period which immediately precedes the second advent, and plainly warns us against the proclamation of the Judgment at hand prior to that time. Here we join issue with our opponents. Instead of finding that the apostles gave this proclamation, as some teach, we shall find indubitable evidence that they located it far in the future, and that they admonished the church to heed none that should precede a given time. If we recur to the book of Acts, we shall find Paul preaching before Felix of the Judgment to come; and before the Athenians, that God hath appointed a day in the which he will judge the world in righteousness by Jesus Christ. Acts 24 : 25 ; 17 : 31. But that book nowhere intimates that Christ was immediately coming to judgment. Peter points his hearers to the future, saying that the heavens which had then received Christ, must retain him until the times of restitution. Acts 3 : 21.

The first Epistle to the Thessalonians may seem to teach that the apostles expected the coming of Christ to judgment in their day. Indeed, it is evident that such an idea was received from it by the Thessalonian church. Hence it was, that in his second Epistle to them, Paul found it necessary to speak explicitly on the point. He tells them that the coming of Christ to the Judgment could not take place until the great apostasy; and as the result of that apostasy, that the man of sin should be revealed, showing himself that he is God, and exalting himself above all that is called God, or that is worshiped. That this mystery of iniquity is the great Romish apostasy, none but a papist will deny.

Paul reminds the Thessalonians that he had told them of these things when he was yet with them. And where could Paul have learned this fact which he had thus stated to them? He was accustomed to reason from the Scriptures, and not to deal in assertion. Hence it is very evident that he refers to the prophecy of Daniel, which in its seventh chapter has given the successive events which intervened between its time and the Judgment. In this series of events it has with wonderful precision described the power to which Paul has referred as the man of sin. No Protestant will deny the identity of Daniel's little horn and Paul's man of sin. And as Daniel has brought it into a series of events which ends with the Judgment and the setting up of the everlasting kingdom, it is an easy matter for Paul to tell where in this series of events he stood, and whether the Judgment was the next event or not. The apostle, therefore, plainly tells them that that day was not at hand. For the man of sin, the little horn, must arise and perform his predicted work; and when that should be accomplished, the coming of Christ should transpire, to consume "that Wicked" with its brightness.

Now, when was the little horn to arise? Daniel was told that it should arise after the ten horns upon the fourth beast; or, in other words, after the fourth empire should be divided into ten kingdoms, which was accomplished about five hundred years after Christ. The Judgment, therefore, could not come prior to that time. But how long was this little horn to have power to wear out the saints?—Daniel informs us that it should be for "a time, and times, and the dividing of time." How long is this period?—

Rev. 12 shows that it is 1260 prophetic days, or years. Verses 6, 14. It follows, therefore, that the apostle carries the mind forward five hundred years, to the development of the man of sin, and thence 1260 years for his triumph, before the Judgment could be preached as an event immediately impending. Whoever will carefully read Dan. 7, will get the original of Paul's argument in 2 Thess. 2, and will not fail to see the force of his statement.

The papal supremacy began in 538, and ended in 1798 with the overthrow of the pope's temporal power. Therefore the warning of Paul against a false proclamation respecting the Judgment at hand, expires at that time, and not before ; for we will then have reached the point of time when the last important event in Dan. 7, before the Judgment, has transpired. An angel from heaven, preaching the hour of God's Judgment come many years in the past, would be giving a different gospel from that preached by Paul. Those who locate the angel of Rev. 14: 6, 7, in past ages, virtually place upon his head the anathema of Paul in Gal. 1 : 8. And, what is of very deep interest, the point of time at which Paul's warning expires, is the commencement of the time of the end,—the very point to which the visions of Daniel were closed up and sealed. Compare Dan. 11: 33, 35 and 7 : 25, and the fact that the 1260 years' persecution of the saints terminates with the commencement of the time of the end, will appear obvious. How gloriously does this view of the subject make the truth of God shine out ! for the warning of the apostle against a false proclamation of the Judgment at hand, expires at the very point where the seal is taken from those prophecies which show when the Judgment sits. And it is respecting this period, the time of the end, that it is said, Many shall run to and fro, and knowledge (on the very subject which was before concealed) shall be increased. Then the time of the end is the period in which the Judgment-hour cry, and the subsequent messages, are to be given. Dan. 8 : 17, 26 ; 12 : 4, 9.

Another important argument on this point is found in what our Lord has said relative to the signs of his second advent. The church were to understand when his coming was at hand, by the fulfillment of certain promised tokens. Until these should be seen, they were not authorized to look for the immediate advent of the Lord. But when the signs which our Lord promised began to appear, his church might then know that his coming to judge the quick and dead was at hand. It is an interesting fact, that Christ has marked the time in which these signs were to begin to appear. Consequently, the messages in question could not be delivered prior to that time. "Immediately after the tribulation of those days shall the sun be darkened, and the moon shall not give her light, and the stars shall fall from heaven, and the powers of the heavens shall be shaken." Matt. 24 : 29. "But in those days, after that tribulation, the sun shall be darkened, and the moon shall not give her light, and the stars of heaven shall fall, and the powers that are in heaven shall be shaken." Mark 13 : 24, 25. We think there can be no mistake that in these scriptures our Lord refers to the papal tribulation of Daniel the prophet. The signs of his second coming were to commence "*in* those days," but "*after* that tribulation." In other words, the 1260 prophetic days would not be quite over, but their tribulation would be ended, when the sun should be darkened. The sun was darkened in 1780, and the tribulation of those days was then past, but the days did not expire till 1798. Thus we have the signs of our Lord's immediate advent just opening upon us, as we come down to the time of the end, the period when the vision should be unsealed, and many run to and fro with the word of warning to a perishing world.

The parable recorded in Matt. 22 : 1–14 and Luke 14 : 16–24, furnishes an important testimony on this subject. Matthew gives a particular account of the first part of this parable, but merely states in a word the final calls to the guests. Luke, on the contrary, omits the first part of the parable, but gives its concluding features with peculiar distinctness. We think the identity of the parables in Matt. 22 and Luke 14 will be seen by every one who will compare those scriptures. It is evident that Matthew, by the calls to dinner, represents the calls which were made to the Jews at the first advent. It is to be observed that the general work of inviting the guests had preceded these calls; for these are a special announcement to those that *had been bidden*, that the dinner is ready. These we understand to refer to the work of John the Baptist and others at the time of the first advent. And we understand that the destruction of the city and people in the parable refers to the destruction of Jerusalem and the rejection of the Jews.

The call to the dinner proving of no effect, the king turns to another people. We understand this as we do the text in which our Lord tells the

Jews that the kingdom should be taken from them, and given to a nation bringing forth the fruits thereof. Matt. 21 : 43. This part of the parable Matthew has given in a word, that the servants in obedience to the command of their Lord were enabled to furnish the wedding with guests. But Luke has taken up this portion with minute accuracy. The dinner indeed was past, and the people to whom it was offered were unworthy of sharing it as guests; but the purpose of the king was not to be made void. At supper time, says Luke, a message was sent forth to announce to those that had been bidden, that supper was ready. We understand that this call to the supper is made to the Gentiles, and that it is in immediate connection with the second advent. For we think that none will deny that the supper of Luke 14 : 16 and that of Rev. 19 : 9 are the same. Thus we see that there was to the Jews the general work of bidding the guests, and the special call at dinner time; and that to the Gentiles there is the general work of the gospel in bidding, and then at supper time the special call to the marriage supper.

These three calls to the marriage supper (Luke 14 : 16–24) we understand to be the same as the three messages of Rev. 14 : 6–12. The first call to the supper is "at supper time," and the first angel announces that "the hour of His judgment is come." None will dispute the fact that the judgment and the marriage supper are in immediate connection with each other. Rev. 19 : 20. The three calls are not the general work of the gospel in bidding; they are made at supper time, that is, at the close of the day. And the three proclamations in Rev. 14, in like manner, are not the general work of the gospel, but special warnings addressed to the world as the great work of our High Priest is closing up.

The book of Nahum furnishes a very striking testimony on this subject. The chariots are to seem like torches, and to run like the lightnings, in the day of God's preparation. Chap. 2. We may learn the event for which this day of preparation is appointed, by reading the first chapter of this prophet. That the sublime scenes of the second advent and the day of God are there portrayed, we think few will be disposed to deny. The day of God's preparation is, therefore, for this very event. Now, it is evident that the hour of God's Judgment cannot precede the day of his preparation for the Judgment. Hence the day of God's preparation is the time for the warning respecting the Judgment, and the associated proclamations to the inhabitants of the earth. And how strikingly have we seen the sign which marks the day of God's preparation fulfilled before our eyes! Since the time of the end commenced, in which the prophecies relative to the Judgment were to be unsealed, and many were to run to and fro, and knowledge to be increased, chariots running like the lightnings have made their appearance in every part of the civilized world. We think this a demonstration that we are now in the day of God's preparation, and that, consequently, this is the period of time in which the three proclamations of Rev. 14 are to be made; for the day of God's preparation for the second advent must be the time for the world to be warned respecting that event.

If we read the message of the second angel with care, and the more full reference to the subject in Rev. 18, we may also gather some important ideas relative to the chronology of these messages. The people of God are called out of Babylon, that the plagues which God is about to inflict upon her may not fall upon them also. These plagues are enumerated as death, mourning, and famine, and utter destruction by fire. And it is said that these shall come upon her in one day. It is evident that these plagues have not yet come upon her. The hour of Babylon's judgment, when the kings shall mourn over her for fear of her torment, is yet future. The warning, therefore, respecting Babylon, must of necessity relate to that generation which shall live when her plagues shall come upon her. The warning respecting the flood, or the destruction of Sodom, belonged to that time which witnessed those events. And the warning respecting the judgments on Babylon must relate to that generation which shall be alive when these judgments are to be inflicted.

The third angel presents a fearful warning against the worship of the beast and his image, and the reception of his mark. It must be evident to every person that this warning must relate to the time when men shall be required to worship the image on pain of death. That this work of the two-horned beast, as recorded in Chap. 13, has as yet been accomplished but in part, is certain. See verses 13–15. Hence it is a great error to locate this proclamation in any past age.

Such are the reasons, in brief, which establish the fact that these proclamations are addressed to the last generation of men. These messages are addressed to men in a state of probation. But it is contrary to the economy of grace that angels should visibly engage in the preaching of the gospel; therefore these angels must symbolize a body of men proclaiming the messages in question; or we may understand that literal angels have the oversight of this work, and that it is carried out through the agency of men.

CHAPTER II.

THE PROCLAMATION OF THE FIRST ANGEL.

Identity of the Angels of Rev. 14: 6 and 10: 1—The Open Book of Chapter 10—Nature of this Proclamation—Time when it is heard—Extent of the Warning—Evidences on which it is based—Reference to John the Baptist—The Disappointment.

"And I saw another angel fly in the midst of heaven, having the everlasting gospel to preach unto them that dwell on the earth, and to every nation, and kindred, and tongue, and people, saying with a loud voice, Fear God, and give glory to him; for the hour of his Judgment is come; and worship him that made heaven and earth, and the sea, and the fountains of waters." Rev. 14: 6, 7.

WE call this the first angel, because it is the first of the series. See verse 9. John calls it "another angel," from the fact that he had previously seen an angel flying through the midst of heaven, after the fourth angel had sounded, announcing the last three trumpets as woe trumpets. See chap. 8: 13. This was about the close of the sixth century, and this fact shows that the first angel of Rev. 14 does not belong to the apostolic age.

We understand that this angel is the same as the one brought to view in Rev. 10. We shall therefore briefly refer to that chapter as explanatory of chap. 14: 6, 7, and as furnishing an important argument respecting the time of its fulfillment. Chap. 9 presents the first and second woes. The prophetic period connected with the second woe terminated with the political power of the Ottoman Empire, Aug. 11, 1840.* Thus ends the ninth chapter, and the tenth opens with the descent of a mighty angel from heaven with a little book in his hand, who cries with a loud voice, as when a lion roareth, and then lifts up his hand to heaven, and swears that time shall be no longer.

This oath cannot mean duration as measured by days and years, for in chap. 20 we have 1000 years measured off between the two resurrections; and, for aught that appears to the contrary, duration will ever be measured thus. Nor can it mean probationary time, for two reasons: 1. It is certain, from verse 7, that this announcement precedes the voice of the seventh angel, and it is in the days of the commencement of his voice that the mystery of God is finished; 2. After this oath of the angel, it is said to John, who doubtless personates the church, that he must prophesy again. These reasons furnish conclusive proof that pro-

---

* See "The Sounding of the Seven Trumpets," published at the *Review and Herald* Office.

bation has not closed when this oath is uttered. Hence we understand that this oath has reference to the prophetic periods, and that this angel with the little book open in his hand is the same as the angel of chap. 14, announcing that the hour of God's Judgment has come. The little book which was open in his hand, we understand to be the prophecy of Daniel, which was to be sealed up until the time of the end. The angel of chap. 10 preached from this little book, and it is this prophecy of Daniel that contains the prophetic time on which the angel of chap. 14: 6 bases his proclamation that the hour of God's Judgment is come.

This proclamation is one of pre-eminent importance. It is not a mere local judgment, but one that concerns all the inhabitants of the earth. Hence it has reference to the final Judgment scene. It is the same gospel that Paul preached that is here styled the "everlasting gospel." But the great truth uttered by this angel would not have been a truth if uttered by Paul; for he lived at the commencement of the gospel dispensation, and this proclamation relates to its closing scenes. It seems to be the same as "this gospel of the kingdom " that our Lord presents in Matt. 24: 14 as the sign of the end of this dispensation.

The truth on this point is well expressed in the following language of the late Sylvester Bliss:—

" As an indication of the approach of the end, there was, however, to be seen another angel flying through the midst of heaven, having the everlasting gospel to preach unto them that dwell on the earth, and to every nation, and kindred, and tongue, and people. Rev. 14: 6. The burden of this angel was to be the *same* gospel which had

been before proclaimed; but connected with it
was the additional motive of the *proximity* of the
kingdom—'saying with a loud voice, Fear God,
and give glory to him; for the hour of his Judgment is come; and worship him that made heaven
and earth, and the sea, and the fountains of waters.' Verse 7. No mere preaching of the gospel,
without announcing its *proximity*, could fulfill
this message." *

We firmly believe that this proclamation has
been made, and that the preaching of the immediate advent of our Lord has been in fulfillment
in this prophecy. Prior to the fall of the Ottoman Empire in 1840, it had been shown by those
who were preaching the immediate advent of
Christ, that the hour, day, month, and year of
Ottoman supremacy would expire the 11th of
August, 1840. When the event verified the
truthfulness of this calculation, the way was prepared for the advent message to go with mighty
power. The prophecies were not only unsealed,
but, in the providence of God, a demonstration of
the truthfulness of the mode of calculation respecting the prophetic times was given to the world.
Thus, at the very time when the mighty angel of
God was to come down with the little book open
in his hand, and to cry with a loud voice, the advent message began to be proclaimed with great
power. It was the good news of the everlasting
kingdom, and of the advent of our glorious King.

Hence it is evident that the advent proclama-
tion comes in at the right time in this prophecy.
The declaration of this angel, that the mystery of
God should be finished in the days of the voice of

---

* *Advent Herald*, Dec. 14, 1850.

the seventh angel, as He had declared to his servants the prophets, presents several important facts : 1. That the angel bases his preaching upon the authority of the prophets ; 2. That the finishing of the mystery of God occupies *days* at the commencement of the voice of the seventh angel, and we understand the days of this angel to be years, as were those of the fifth and sixth angels of chap. 9 ; 3. That it shall be finished in the days of the voice of the seventh angel in the manner that the prophets have declared. One of them, Daniel, has told how the mystery of God should be finished at the end of the 2300 days ; viz., the Sanctuary should be cleansed, which event accomplishes the work of our great High Priest.

The extent of this proclamation is worthy of notice. An English writer, Mourant Brock, thus remarks :—

" It is not merely in great Britain that the expectation of the near return of the Redeemer is entertained, and the voice of warning raised, but also in America, India, and on the continent of Europe. In America, about three hundred ministers of the word are thus preaching ' this gospel of the kingdom ; ' while in this country, about seven hundred of the Church of England are raising the same cry."*

Dr. Joseph Wolfe traveled in Arabia Felix, through the region inhabited by the descendants of Hobab, Moses' father-in-law. In Yemen, he saw a book which he mentions thus :—

"The *Arabs* of this place have a book called Seera, which treats of the *second coming of*

---

* " Advent Tracts," vol. ii. p. 135.

Christ, and his reign in glory! In Yemen, he spent six days with the Rechabites. 'They drink no wine, plant no vineyards, sow no seed, live in tents, and remember the words of Jonadab, the son of Rechab.' With them were children of Israel, of the tribe of Dan, who reside near Terim in Hatramawt, *who expect, in common with the children of Rechab, the speedy arrival of the Messiah in the clouds of heaven.*" *

The "Voice of the Church," by D. T. Taylor, speaks as follows concerning the wide diffusion of the advent sentiment :—

"In Wirtemberg there is a Christian colony numbering hundreds, who look for the speedy advent of Christ ; also another of like belief on the shores of the Caspian ; the Molokaners, a large body of dissenters from the Russian Greek Church, residing on the shores of the Baltic,—a very pious people of whom it is said, 'Taking the Bible alone for their creed, the *norm* of their faith is simply the Holy Scriptures,'—are characterized by the 'expectation of Christ's immediate and visible reign upon earth.' In Russia, the doctrine of Christ's coming and reign is preached to some extent, and received by many of the lower class. It has been extensively agitated in Germany, particularly in the south part among the Moravians. In Norway, charts and books on the advent have been circulated extensively, and the doctrine has been received by many. Among the Tartars in Tartary, there prevails an expectation of Christ's advent about this time. English and American publications on this doctrine have been sent to Holland, Germany, India, Ireland, Con-

---

* Wolfe's "Mission to Bokhara."

stantinople, Rome, and to nearly every missionary station on the globe. At the Turks Islands, it has been received to some extent among the Wesleyans.

"Mr. Fox, a Scottish missionary to the Teloogoo people, was a believer in Christ's soon coming. James MacGregor Bertram, a Scottish missionary of the Baptist order at St. Helena, has sounded the cry extensively on that island, making many converts and pre-millennialists; he has also preached it at South Africa at the missionary stations there. David N. Lord informs us that a large proportion of the missionaries who have gone from Great Britain to make known the gospel to the heathen, and who are now laboring in Asia and Africa, are millennarians; and Joseph Wolfe, D. D., according to his journals, between the years 1821 and 1845 proclaimed the Lord's speedy advent in Palestine, Egypt, on the shores of the Red Sea, Mesopotamia, the Crimea, Persia, Georgia, throughout the Ottoman Empire, in Greece, Arabia, Turkistan, Bokhara, Afghanistan, Cashmere, Hindoostan, Thibet, in Holland, Scotland, and Ireland, at Constantinople, Jerusalem, St. Helena, also on shipboard in the Mediterranean, and at New York City to all denominations. He declares he has preached among Jews, Turks, Mohammedans, Parsees, Hindoos, Chaldeans, Yescedes, Syrians, Sabeans, to pashas, sheiks, shahs, the kings of Organtsh and Bokhara, the queen of Greece, etc.; and of his extraordinary labors the *Investigator* says, 'No individual has, perhaps, given greater publicity to the doctrine of the second coming of the Lord Jesus Christ than has this well-known missionary to the world. Wherever he goes, he proclaims the approaching advent of the Messiah in glory.'"*

None can deny that this world-wide warning of impending judgment has been given. The nature of the evidence adduced in its support now claims our attention, as furnishing the most conclusive testimony that it was a message from Heaven.

All the great outlines of the world's prophetic history were shown to be complete in the present generation. The great prophetic chain of Dan. 2, also the chains of chaps. 7, 8 and 11, 12, were shown to be just accomplished. The same was true of our Lord's prophetic description of the gospel dispensation. Matt. 24 ; Mark 13 ; Luke 21. The prophetic periods of Dan. 7, 8, 9, 12 and Rev. 11, 12, 13, were shown to harmonize with, and to unitedly sustain, this great proclamation. The signs in the heavens and upon the earth and sea, in the church and among the nations, with one voice bore witness to the warning which God addressed to the human family. Joel 2 : 30, 31 ; Matt. 24 :-29–31 ; Mark 13 : 24–26 ; Luke 21 : 25–36 ; 2 Tim. 3 ; 2 Pet. 3 ; Rev. 6 : 12, 13. And besides the mighty array of evidence on which this warning was based, the great outpouring of the Holy Spirit in connection with this proclamation set the seal of Heaven to its truth.

The warning of John the Baptist, which was to prepare the way for the first advent of our Lord, was of short duration, and limited in its extent. For each prophetic testimony which sustained the work of John, we have several which support the proclamation of Christ's near

---

* Wolfe's "Mission to Bokhara," pp. 342–344.

advent. John had not the aid of the press to disseminate his proclamation, nor the facility of modern methods of travel; he was a humble man, dressed in camel's hair, and he performed no miracles. If the Pharisees and lawyers rejected the counsel of God against themselves, in not being baptized of John, how great must be the guilt of those who reject the warning sent by God to prepare the way of the second advent!

But those were disappointed who expected the Lord in 1843 and '44. This fact is with many a sufficient reason for rejecting all the testimony in this case. We acknowledge the disappointment, but cannot acknowledge that this furnishes a just reason for denying the hand of God in this work. The Jewish Church were disappointed when at the close of the work of John the Baptist, Jesus presented himself as the promised Messiah; and the trusting disciples were most sadly disappointed when He whom they expected to deliver Israel was by wicked hands taken and slain. And after his resurrection, when they expected him to restore again the kingdom to Israel, they could not but be disappointed when they understood that he was going away to his Father, and that they were to be left for a long season to tribulation and anguish. But disappointment does not prove that God has no hand in the guidance of his people. It should lead them to correct their errors, but it should not lead them to cast away their confidence in God. It was because the children of Israel were disappointed in the wilderness that they so often denied their guidance as divine. They are set forth as an admonition to us, that we should not fall after the same example of unbelief.

But it must be apparent to every student of the Scriptures, that the angel who proclaims the hour of God's Judgment does not give the latest message of mercy. Rev. 14 presents two other and later proclamations, before the close of human probation. This fact alone is sufficient to prove that the coming of the Lord does not take place until the second and third proclamations have been added to the first. The same thing may also be seen in the fact that after the angel of chap. 10 has sworn that time shall be no longer, another work of prophesying before many people and nations is announced. Hence we understand that the first angel preaches the hour of God's Judgment come; that is, he preaches the termination of the prophetic periods, and that this is the time which he swears shall be no longer.

The Judgment does, of necessity, commence before the advent of Christ; for he comes to execute the Judgment (Jude 14, 15; Matt. 25 : 31–46; John 5 : 27); and at the sound of the last trumpet, he confers immortality upon every one of the righteous, and passes by all the wicked. The investigative Judgment does, therefore, precede the execution of the same by the Saviour. It is the province of the Father to preside in this investigative work, as set forth in Dan. 7. At this tribunal, the Son closes up his work as high priest, and is crowned king. Thence he comes to earth to execute the decisions of his Father. It is this work of judgment by the Father which the first angel introduces.

The great period of 2300 days, which was the most important period in marking the definite time in that proclamation, extends to the cleansing of the Sanctuary. That the cleansing of the

Sanctuary is not the cleansing of any part of the earth, but that it is the last work of our great High Priest in the heavenly Tabernacle, before his advent to the earth, has been clearly shown.* And we understand that it is while the work of cleansing the Sanctuary takes place that the latest message of mercy is proclaimed. Thus it will be seen that the prophetic periods, and the proclamation which is based upon them, do not extend to the coming of the Lord.

---

* See " The Prophecy of Daniel," published at the *Review and Herald* Office.

CHAPTER III.

THE PROCLAMATION OF THE SECOND ANGEL.

Time of this Proclamation—Derivation of the term Babylon—
Babylon not the Wicked World—Not the City of Rome—Ex-
planation of Symbols—The Seven Heads of the Beast—
Rome the Seat of the Beast—Babylon not a Literal City
Meaning of the Symbol—Facts which identify Protestants as
a part of this Great City.

"And there fol-
lowed another an-
gel, saying, Babylon
is fallen, is fallen,
that great city be-
cause she made all
nations drink of the
wine of the wrath of
her fornication."
Rev. 14 : 8.

THE first important inquiry relates to the time
when this proclamation is to be made. As this
angel follows the one who proclaims the hour of
God's Judgment, it is evident that this proclamation is the next event in order. And as it has
been shown that the proclamation of the hour of
God's Judgment is addressed to those who live in
the last days, it is certain that the Second Angel's
Message belongs to the same time, and that it was
not fulfilled centuries in the past. And the fact
that at the time when this proclamation of the
fall of Babylon is made, the plagues and utter destruction of Babylon, which came under the seventh vial, are then immediately impending, is
also conclusive proof that this proclamation belongs to the last days. Rev. 18 : 1–10; 16 · 17–

21. We conclude, therefore, that the generation that shall be alive when the plagues are poured out on Babylon, is the one to which the Second Angel's Message is addressed.

Our next inquiry relates to the meaning of the term *Babylon.* What is designated by the word *Babylon* in the book of Revelation ?

The word *Babylon* signifies confusion, and is derived from *Babel,* the place where God confounded the inhabitants of the earth in their impious attempt to build a tower up to heaven. Gen. 11 : 9, margin ; 10 : 10, margin. The word, being the chosen term of the Holy Spirit to designate "that mighty city" which is so prominently noticed in the book of Revelation, was doubtless selected with especial reference to its signification, and to the circumstances that originated the word. That Babylon does not comprise the whole wicked world, and that it does not consist of some one literal city, but that it is composed of professed worshipers of God, we think can be clearly shown. This is not an abstract question, but is eminently practical, and is intimately connected with our duty toward God.

BABYLON IS NOT THE WHOLE WICKED WORLD,

Rev. 17 represents Babylon by the symbol of a woman seated on a scarlet-colored beast. If, therefore, the woman Babylon represents the whole of this fallen world, the entire empire of the Devil, what does the beast represent upon which the woman is seated ? Is it not a fact that the beast represents the fourth empire of our earth in its papal form ? And, that being the case, is it not a certainty that Babylon does not include the whole wicked world ? That the beast and the woman are two distinct symbols, is evident from verse 7.

The same chapter represents the unlawful connection of Babylon with the kings of the earth, and that she has made the inhabitants of the earth drunken. She is also represented as that great city that reigneth over the kings of the earth. Babylon is therefore distinct from the kings of the earth, and does not include all the wicked of the earth.

It is also stated that this great harlot sat upon many waters. In the explanation it is stated that these waters are peoples, and multitudes, and nations, and tongues. Rev. 17 : 1, 15. Certainly we should not confound the harlot with the waters or nations upon which she is said to sit. When Babylon is destroyed, being thrown down as a millstone is cast into the mighty deep, and utterly burned with fire, the kings of the earth, the merchants, the sailors, etc., are still spared, and mourn, and lament over her. It is plain, therefore, that the utter destruction of Babylon is not the destruction of those wicked men who have lived in iniquity with her. Hence it follows that Babylon does not comprise the whole wicked world.

BABYLON NOT THE CITY OF ROME.

As some have strongly advocated the view that Rome is the Babylon of the book of Revelation, we will examine the reasons that are adduced in support of this view. The argument stands thus :—

The angel told John that the woman which he had seen was the great city which reigned over the kings of the earth, and that the seven heads of the beast were seven mountains upon which the woman sat. The explanation of "the mystery of the woman" is regarded as decisive testimony that Rome is the Babylon of the book of Revelation. To the foregoing reasons some add the statement that a woman is used in every other instance in the book of Revelation as the symbol of a literal city, and consequently must mean a literal city in this case. But we are compelled to dissent from this view, for the following reasons:—

The grand principle assumed by the foregoing view is this : The interpretation of a symbol must always be literal, and can never consist in the substitution of one symbol for another ; and hence the interpretation of the woman as a city, and of the heads of the beasts as mountains upon which the woman sitteth, must be literal. That there are exceptions to this rule, and that the case in question furnishes a manifest exception, we will now show. In Rev. 11 : 3 the two witnesses are introduced. The next verse is an explanation of what is meant by the two witnesses : " These are the two olive-trees, and the two candlesticks standing before the God of the earth." There can be no question that in this case the explanation of the symbol consists in the substitution of other symbols. In other words, the explanation consists in transferring the meaning to other symbols, which are elsewhere clearly explained.

That this is the case in Rev. 17, we will now show. The angel introduces his explanation of the heads by saying, " Here is the mind which hath wisdom," plainly implying that wisdom was needed in order to understand what he was there communicating. With the fact before us, that in Rev. 11 the explanation consists in substituting one symbol for another, and with the caution of the angel, as he gives the explanation in this case, let us consider what he utters :—

"The seven heads are seven mountains, on which the woman sitteth." "The woman which thou sawest is that great city, which reigneth over the kings of the earth." Verses 9, 18. The wisdom which is needed to rightly comprehend the words of the angel, would doubtless lead us to compare the different instances in which the same facts are referred to in the book of Revelation. If we do this, the following points will appear :—

1. Chap. 13 informs us that one of these seven heads was wounded unto death, and that this deadly wound was healed. Or, as the same fact is stated again, it had a wound by a sword, and did live. It would be utter folly to assert this of a literal mountain. Hence the heads are not mountains of earth.

2. Each of the seven heads is represented in chap. 12 with a crown upon it, even as each of the ten horns is thus represented in chap. 13. Each of the heads must therefore represent a kingdom or government, even as the horns represent governments.

3. It is evident that the seven heads are successive (that is, the beast has but one head at a time), in distinction from the ten horns, which are contemporary. But the seven hills of Rome are not successive ; for it cannot be said of them, "Five are fallen, and one is, and the other is not

yet come ; and when he cometh, he must continue a short space." The beast itself is the eighth, and is of the seven, which proves that the beast is a literal mountain, or that the heads are not.

4. The heads of the beast must, according to Dan. 7: 6 compared with Dan. 8: 22, be explained as kingdoms or governments. Mountains, according to Dan. 2: 35, 44 and Jer. 51: 25, denote kingdoms. But the version of Prof. Whiting, which is a literal translation of the text, removes all obscurity from Rev. 17: 9, 10: "The seven heads are seven mountains on which the woman sitteth, and they are seven kings." Thus it will be seen that the angel represents the heads as mountains, and then explains the mountains to be seven successive kings. Thus we see that the angel transferred the meaning from one symbol to another, and then gave the explanation of the second symbol.

Having proved that the mountains are not literal, but symbolic, it follows that the woman who sits upon them cannot represent a literal city; for a literal city cannot sit upon symbolic mountains. Hence it appears that the angel transfers the meaning from one symbol to another, as in verses 9, 10; chap. 11: 4. And it is certain that the woman of chap. 12 represents the church, and not a literal city. Therefore it is a mistaken idea that a woman in the book of Revelation, as a symbol, always represents a literal city.

Another evidence that the city of Rome is not the Babylon of the Apocalypse, is found in the following important fact: Rome was and is "the seat of the beast;" therefore the city of Rome cannot be the woman seated upon the beast; for Rome cannot be both the seat of the beast and the woman that sits upon the beast. Lest any should deny that Rome is the seat of the beast, we will prove that point from the New Testament. The seat of the beast is the same that had been the seat of the dragon. Rev. 13:2. This dragon is the power that ruled the world at the time of our Saviour's birth. Rev. 12. Consequently it is imperial Rome. The seat of the imperial power, the throne of the Cæsars, was at Rome in Italy. Luke 2:1; Acts 25:10–12, 21; compared with Acts 26:32; 27:1, 24; 28:14–16. The fact being established that Rome is the seat of the beast, it follows that Rome is not the woman Babylon, seated upon the beast.

The fact that Rome is not the Babylon of the Apocalypse may also be demonstrated from Rev. 16. The fifth vial is poured out upon the seat of the beast, which we have shown to be Rome. But the great city, Babylon, does not receive her cup of wrath until the seventh vial is poured out. Verses 10, 11, 17–19. Then Babylon and Rome are not the same.

Were Babylon a literal city, but few, at most, of the people of God could be found in it, and but a portion of any class of the wicked; so that almost all of every class of men would in that case be outside of the Babylon of Revelation.

But it is very evident that at the time of the cry, "Come out of her, my people," the people of God, as a body, are in that great city. It is also worthy of notice that if Babylon is a literal city, it must be a place of the greatest commercial importance; for in Rev. 18 it is represented as the great center of commerce, and its destruction causes universal mourning among the merchants and sailors of the world. It is certain that Rome is as far from being a commercial city as any one upon the globe; and the destruction of Rome would not in the slightest degree affect commercial business.

"At Rome," says Gibbon, "commerce was always held in contempt." Nor could the sailors and ship-masters of the earth lament over her, saying, "What city is like unto this great city!" for either New York or London is equal to a great number of such cities as Rome in commercial importance. And, indeed, there is not a city upon the globe whose destruction would cause all commerce to cease, and all the sailors and merchants of the earth to mourn. These arguments, we think, demonstrate that Rome is not the Babylon of the Apocalypse.

BABYLON A SYMBOL OF THE PROFESSED CHURCH UNITED TO THE WORLD.

Babylon is the name of the symbolic harlot which was seen by John. A woman is the symbol of a church. Rev. 12. A harlot is the symbol of a corrupt church. Eze. 16. It is evident that the woman in Rev. 17 should be interpreted in the same manner as the one in chap. 12. As that symbol undoubtedly represents the true church, though spoken of as a woman and her seed, so the harlot and her daughters are doubtless the entire corrupt church. Rev. 18:5. We understand, therefore, that Babylon is not limited to a single ecclesiastical body; but that its very name renders it necessary that it should be composed of many.

If the harlot to whom the kings of the earth have unlawfully united themselves, symbolizes only the Church of Rome, it follows that many of the wicked powers of the earth are quite free from this sin. The Greek Church is the established church of Russia and Greece; the Lutheran Church is the established Church of Prussia, Holland, Sweden, Norway, and a part of the smaller German states; England has Episcopacy for her State religion; and other countries have their established religions, and zealously oppose dissenters. Babylon has made all the nations drunk with her wine; it can therefore symbolize nothing less than the universal worldly church.

It will be seen, therefore, that we do not exclusively apply the prophecy respecting Babylon to any one of the corrupt bodies which have existed, or which now exist. In this great city of confusion, we understand that the corrupt Roman and Greek churches occupy a large space, and act an important part. War, oppression, conformity to the world, and the like, identify with sad and faithful accuracy the great body of the Protestant churches as an important constituent part of this great Babylon.

When the papal church possessed the power, it destroyed a vast multitude of the saints of God. Nor has the Protestant Church, since its rise, been free from acts of persecution whenever it has possessed the power to perform them. The Protestants of Geneva, with John Calvin at their head, burned Michael Servetus, a man who had barely escaped the same fate at the hands of the popish inquisition. They did this for the same reason that the papists do the like; that is, they did it for a difference of opinion, and because they had the power to do it. Witness also the long-continued oppression which the Church of England was able to maintain toward all dissenters.

Even the puritan fathers of New England, themselves fugitives from the wicked oppression of the Church of England, could not forbear to hang the Quakers, and to whip and imprison the Baptists. In all these cases the civil arm was under the control of these professed worshipers of Jehovah, and they could not forbear to use it.

The Protestant Church, till within a short time, held many thousand slaves ; nor is the fact to be disguised that the professed church was the right arm of the slave power. Nor was slavery abolished by the churches. To the secular power falls the honor of overthrowing this gigantic evil; and the churches have never confessed their great wrong in so long upholding this iniquitous system. This great fact identifies the Protestant Church as a part of Babylon, with absolute certainty. Rev. 18 : 13. The celebrated Albert Barnes, whose notes on the New Testament are so widely diffused, uses the following startling language : "There is no power out of the church that could sustain slave y an hour, if it were not sustained in it." "The churches are the bulwark of American slavery."

Christ forbade his people to lay up treasures on earth (Matt. 6 : 19); but the professed church at the present day, as a body, exhibits greater eagerness in the pursuit of 'wealth, and in the acquisition of Babylonish treasures (Rev. 18 : 11–14), than even worldlings themselves. In exposing the corruption of the Babylonish church of his time, Christ warned his own people to beware of the like abominations. "But be not ye called Rabbi," says Christ; that is, master, or doctor; "for one is your Master, even Christ; and all ye are brethren." Matt. 23 : 8. Apparently to imitate the Romish Church, Protestants call their ministers Reverend. This word, which is used only once in the Scriptures, is there applied to God. Ps. 111 : 9. If it is a sin for the church to call her ministers Rabbi, or master, how much greater sin must it be for her to apply to them the title of Reverend, which belongs to God alone! Not content with this, some of these professed servants of Jesus Christ become Right Reverend, and Very Reverend. And not a few of them become Doctors of Divinity, so great is their proficiency in the doctrines of Christ!

The New Testament speaks in the most decisive manner respecting plainness of dress; but the majority of the professed church at the present time walk in all the fashionable follies of life. They are arrayed in all the gaudy attire of Babylonian merchandise. The merchants of Babylon are the great men of the earth. In the fold of the nominal church is to be found a large portion of the lawyers, doctors, politicians, and great men of the world. To succeed in business, to become honorable in society, or to rise to high offices in the nation, it is very important to make a profession of religion, and to have a good and regular standing in the church. This is most abominable in the sight of God; and yet it is very apparent that the church joyfully welcomes such members, because they will make the body more honorable.

It may be said that even corrupt Protestants should not be joined with Romanists, as forming the great city Babylon; for although Romanists claim infallibility, Protestants never yet have done this. We answer that in this the difference exists only in name. To speak in the language of their several pretensions, Romanists never *can* err; Protestants never *do* err. If Romanists claim infallibility in *advance* for the decrees and ordinances of their church, it is also true that Protestant bodies never *afterward* acknowledge wherein their churches or their councils have been in error. So that Protestant churches have all the advantage of infallibility, and leave to the Romanists all the odium of claiming it.

Babylon is represented as trafficking in the souls of men. Look at the Church of England. There the vacant parishes are in some cases even set up for sale, and the highest bidder becomes the possessor of its revenue and the pastor of its people! To come nearer home, let us look at the various religious denominations in every place where they have sufficient wealth and strength to become popular. They must erect a splendid house of worship, and furnish it in the most expensive style; and the members of the church must dress in all the fashion and pride of life. Then they must have an eloquent man to preach smooth things to fashionable ears. The church which can outdo the others in these particulars will succeed in securing the fashionable sinners of the place as permanent members of the congregation.

The word *Babylon*, as we have seen, signifies confusion, and comes from *Babel*, the place where men, in their impious attempt to build a tower that should reach unto heaven, had their language confounded. Gen. 11. The church should be a unit. This was the will of Christ. Witness his intercession with the Father, as recorded in John 17. He prayed that his disciples might be one, as he and his Father are one; for this would cause the world to believe in Christ. Since the great apostasy, the majority of his professed followers have busied themselves in attempting to climb up to heaven some other way. They have been confounded in the attempt, and scattered abroad upon the face of the earth, with creeds as discordant as the languages of those who were dispersed at the ancient tower. The Holy Spirit uses the word *Babylon* on account of its signification, and it is a most appropriate designation for the great city of confusion to which it is applied.

The church was represented as a chaste virgin, espoused to Christ. 2 Cor. 11 : 2. She became a harlot by seeking the friendship of the world. James 4:4. It was this unlawful connection with the kings of the earth that constituted her the great harlot of the Apocalypse. Rev. 17. The Jewish Church, represented as espoused to the Lord (Jer. 2; 3; 31:32), became a harlot in the same manner. Eze. 16. Even the term *Sodom*, which in Rev. 11 is applied to "the great city," is in Isa. 1 applied to the Jewish Church thus apostatized from God. The fact that Babylon is distinct from, though unlawfully united with, the kings of the earth, is positive proof that Babylon is not the civil power. The fact that the people of God are in her midst just before her overthrow, proves that she is a professedly religious body. We think it must be apparent, therefore, that the Babylon of Rev. 17 symbolizes the professed church unlawfully united to the world.

CHAPTER IV.

THE FALL OF BABYLON.

The Fall of Babylon not the Burning of Rome—Not the Loss of her Civil Power—It is a Moral Fall—The Wine of Babylon—The Churches tested by the First Proclamation—Connection of the First and Second Messages—Testimonies relative to the Fallen State of the Churches—Recent Revivals—Spiritualism as a Confirmation of the Views here Presented—Destruction of Babylon—Duty of God's People.

WHAT constitutes the fall of Babylon? Those who contend that the Babylon of Revelation is the city of Rome, answer that the fall of Babylon is the burning of Rome; while those who make Babylon a symbol of the Church of Rome only, answer that this fall is the loss of her civil power, —the fall of the woman from the beast. We dissent from both these positions, believing that the fall of Babylon is a moral fall, and that it denotes her rejection, as a body, of God. That the fall of Babylon is not the burning of Rome, appears from the following facts:—

1. The cry, "Come out of her, my people," is made after the announcement that she has fallen. Rev. 18 : 2, 4. It is therefore evident that Babylon exists after her fall, and that the people of God are still in her midst; therefore her fall must be distinct from her destruction.

2. When it is said, "Come out of her, my people," it is added as a reason, "that ye be not partakers of her sins, and that ye receive not of her plagues." Her fall had taken place; but she still existed to sin against God, and her plagues were yet future; therefore her fall and her destruction were events entirely distinct.

3. When her plagues are named in verse 8, they are said to be death, mourning, and famine, and utter destruction by fire. Her plagues were yet future at the time of her fall; consequently her fall is not her destruction by fire. Between those two events the people of God make their escape from her.

4. The burning of Rome would not cause that city to become the hold of foul spirits and the cage of every unclean and hateful bird. Indeed, the only effectual cleansing that wicked city will ever receive will be by fire. These facts clearly evince that the fall of Babylon is not the burning of Rome. Besides this, we have clearly proved that Rome is not the Babylon of the Apocalypse, which is sufficient of itself on this point.

That the fall of Babylon is not the loss of civil power by the Papal Church, the following facts clearly prove :—

1. This would make the angel say, Babylon is fallen, that is, has lost her civil power, because she made all nations drink of her wine. Such a statement would be false; for it was by this very means that she obtained her power.

2. Babylon becomes the hold of every foul spirit and the cage of every unclean and hateful bird in consequence of her fall. Rev. 18 : 1, 2. It would be absurd to represent this as the consequence of her loss of civil power.

3. The loss of civil power is not the fall of Babylon, for this would not make her more sinful than before, nor would such a fall as this furnish a reason why the people of God should leave her.

We understand that the fall of Babylon is her rejection by God, that the Holy Spirit leaves her in consequence of her alienation from God and her union with the world, and that thus she is left to the spirits of devils. As an illustration, we will refer to the fall of the Jewish Church, the harlot of Eze. 16. This fall is distinctly stated in Rom. 11. Its particulars may be gathered from Matt. 21 : 43 ; 23 ; 12 : 43–45.

That her fall was her rejection by God, her destruction being deferred for a considerable period, the following facts prove :—

1. The nature of the reasons assigned for the fall of Babylon proves that it is a moral fall ; for it is because she has made the nations drunk with her wine. In other words, it is her wickedness that has caused God to reject her.

2. The consequences of her fall testify that that fall is her rejection by God, and not her destruction ; for her fall causes her to become the hold of foul spirits, and the cage of unclean and hateful birds. This shows that God has given her up to strong delusions. It is for this reason that the voice from heaven cries, " Come out of her, my people." The cause of the fall of Babylon is thus stated : " She made all nations drink of the wine of the wrath of her fornication." Her fornication was her unlawful union with the kings of the earth ; and the wine is that with which the church has intoxicated the nations of the earth. There is but one thing that this can refer to ; viz., false doctrine. This harlot, in consequence of her unlawful union with the powers of the earth, has corrupted the pure truths of the Bible, and with the wine of her false doctrine has intoxicated the nations. A few instances of her corruption of the truths of the Bible must suffice :—

1. The doctrine of a thousand years of peace

and prosperity before the coming of the Lord. This doctrine will probably prove the ruin of as many souls as any heresy that ever cursed the church.

2. The corruption of the ordinance of baptism. Burial in baptism is the divinely authorized memorial of our Lord's burial and resurrection. This has been changed to sprinkling, or pouring, the fitting memorial of but one thing ; viz., the folly and presumption of man.

3. The change of the fourth commandment. The pagan festival of Sunday has been substituted by the church for the rest-day of the Lord. The Bible plainly teaches that the sanctified rest-day of the Lord is the divinely authorized memorial of the rest of Jehovah from the work of creation. But the church has changed this to the first day of the week, to make it a memorial of our Lord's resurrection, in the place of baptism, which has been changed to sprinkling.

4. The doctrine of the natural immortality of the soul. This was derived from the pagan mythology, and was introduced into the church by means of distinguished converts from paganism, who became "fathers of the church." This doctrine makes man's last foe—death—the gate to endless joy, and leaves the resurrection as a thing of minor importance. It is the foundation of modern Spiritualism.

5. The doctrine of the saints' inheritance beyond the bounds of time and space. For this fable, multitudes have turned from the scriptural view of the everlasting kingdom in the new earth.

6. The spiritual second advent. It is well known that the great majority of religious teachers and commentators of the present time openly

advocate the view that Christ's second advent, as brought to view in Matt. 24, took place at the destruction of Jerusalem ; and also that he comes the second time whenever any person dies.

7. Until the time when slavery was forcibly abolished, the institution was upheld in the most confident manner from the Old and New Testaments, by some of the leading doctors of divinity of most denominations; and some of the most distinguished and skillful even tried to find authority for it in the golden rule.

8. Finally, the lowering of the standard of godliness to the dust. This has been carried so far that the multitudes are made to believe that "every one that saith, Lord, Lord, shall enter into the kingdom of heaven." In proof of this, I might appeal to almost every tombstone or funeral discourse.

God appointed the church to be the light of the world, and at the same time ordained that his word should be the light of the church. But when the church becomes unfaithful to her trust, and corrupts the pure doctrines of the gospel, as a natural consequence the world becomes intoxicated with her false doctrine. That the nations of the earth are in such a condition at the present time, is too obvious to be denied. The world is intoxicated in the pursuit of riches and honor, but the sin lies at the door of the church; for the church sanctions what the Lord strictly forbade, and she sets the example to the world. If the church had not intoxicated the world with the wine of her false doctrines, the plain truths of the Bible would powerfully move the public mind. But the world seems hopelessly drunken with the wine of Babylon.

At the time of the First Angel's Message, the people of God were in Babylon; for the announcement of the fall of Babylon, and the cry, "Come out of her, my people," is made after the first proclamation has been heard. Here also we have a most decisive testimony that Babylon includes Protestant as well as Catholic churches. It is certain that the people of God, at the time of the preaching of the hour of his Judgment, were in all the popular churches; and this fact is a most striking testimony as to what constitutes the great city of confusion. In a word, Paul has well described the Babylon of the Apocalypse, and the duty of the people of God with reference to it, in 2 Tim. 3:1-5: "This know also, that in the last days perilous times shall come; for men shall be lovers of their own selves, covetous, boasters, proud, blasphemers, disobedient to parents, un-thankful, unholy, without natural affection, truce-breakers, false accusers, incontinent, fierce, de-spisers of those that are good, traitors, heady, high-minded, lovers of pleasures more than lovers of God; having a form of godliness, but denying the power thereof; *from such turn away.*" Who would dare to limit this description to the Cath-olic Church?

The preaching of the hour of God's Judgment and the immediate coming of the Lord, was at once the test of the church, and the means by which she might have been healed. It was the test of the church in that it showed that her heart was with the world, and not with her Lord; for when the evidences of his immediate advent were set before her, she rejected the tidings with scorn, and cleaved still closer unto the world. But it might have been the means of healing her.

Had she received it, what a work would it have wrought for her? Her unscriptural hope of a temporal reign, her false view of the second advent, her unrighteous justification of oppression and wickedness, her pride and conformity to the world, would all have been swept away. Alas! that this warning from Heaven was rejected!

The last means that Heaven had in store to heal Babylon having failed, God gave her up to her own heart's desire.

It is well known that in immediate connection with the proclamation of the hour of God's Judgment, the announcement of the fall of Babylon was everywhere made throughout our land. Its connection with the advent message is well expressed by the following from Elder Himes, dated McConnellsville, O., Aug. 29, 1844:—

"When we commenced the work of giving the 'midnight cry' with Bro. Miller, in 1840, he had been lecturing nine years. During that time he stood almost alone. But his labors had been incessant and effectual in awakening professors of religion to the true hope of God's people, and the necessary preparation for the advent of the Lord, as also the awakening of all classes of the unconverted to a sense of their lost condition, and the duty of immediate repentance and conversion to God as a preparation to meet the Bridegroom in peace at his coming. These were the great objects of his labor. He made no attempt to convert men to a sect or party, in religion. Hence he labored among all parties and sects without interfering with their organization or discipline, believing that the members of the different communions could retain their standing, and at the same time prepare for the advent of their King and labor for the salvation of men in these relations until the consummation of their hope. When we were persuaded of the truth of the proclamation that the advent was at hand, and embraced the doctrine publicly, we entertained the same views and pursued the same course among the different sects, where we were called in the providence of God to labor. We told the ministers and churches that it was no part of our business to break them up, or to divide and distract them. We had one *distinct object*, and that was to give the 'cry,' the warning of the 'Judgment at the door,' and to persuade our fellow-men to get ready for the event. Most of the ministers and churches that opened their doors to us and our brethren who were proclaiming the advent doctrine, co-operated with us till the last year. The ministry and membership who availed themselves of our labors, but *had not* sincerely embraced the doctrine, saw that they must either go with the doctrine, and preach and maintain it, or in the *crisis* which was right upon them, they would have difficulty with the *decided and determined believers*. They therefore decided against the doctrine, and determined, some by one policy and some by another, to suppress the subject. This placed our brethren and sisters among them in a most trying position. Most of them loved their churches, and could not think of leaving. But when they were ridiculed, oppressed, and in various ways cut off from their former privileges and enjoyment, and when the 'meat in due season' was withheld from them, and the siren song of 'peace and safety' was resounded in their ears from Sabbath to Sabbath, they were soon weaned from their party predilections, and arose in the

majesty of their strength, shook off the yoke, and
raised the cry, ' *Come out of her, my people!* '
This state of things placed us in a trying position,
1. Because we were near the end of our prophetic
time in which we expected the Lord would gather
all his people in one; and 2. We had always
preached a different doctrine, and now that the
circumstances had changed, it would be regarded
as dishonest in us if we should unite in the *cry of
separation* and breaking up of churches that had
received us and our message. We therefore hesi-
tated, and continued to act on our first position
until the church and ministry carried the matter
so far that we were obliged, in the fear of God, to
take a position in defense of the truth and the
down-trodden children of God."*

The testimonies of the churches in 1844, relative to their fallen condition, are worthy of particular notice.

The *Christian Palladium* for May 15, 1844,
speaks in the following mournful strain: "In
every direction we hear the dolorous sound, waft-
ing upon every breeze of heaven, chilling as the
blasts from the icebergs of the north, settling like
an incubus on the breasts of the timid, and
drinking up the energies of the weak,—that
lukewarmness, division, anarchy, and desolation
are distressing the borders of Zion."

The *Religious Telescope* of 1844 uses the following language: "We have never witnessed
such a general declension of religion as at the
present. Truly, the church should awake, and
search into the cause of this affliction; for as an
affliction every one who loves Zion must view it.

Advent Herald, 1844.

When we call to mind how 'few and far between' cases of true conversion are, and the almost unparalleled impenitence and hardness of sinners, we almost involuntarily exclaim, 'Has God forgotten to be gracious? or is the door of mercy closed?'"

About that time, proclamations of fasts and seasons of prayer for the return of the Holy Spirit were sent out in the religious papers. Even the Philadelphia *Sun*, of Nov. 11, 1844, has the following: "The undersigned ministers and members of various denominations in Philadelphia and vicinity, solemnly believing that the present signs of the times—the spiritual dearth in our *churches generally*, and the extreme evils in the world around us—seem to call loudly on all Christians for *a special season of prayer*, do therefore hereby agree, by divine permission, to unite in a *week of special prayer to Almighty God*, for the outpouring of his Holy Spirit on our city, our country, and the world."

Prof. Finney, editor of the Oberlin *Evangelist*, Feb., 1844, says: "We have had the facts before our minds that, in general, the Protestant churches of our country, as such, were either apathetic or hostile to nearly all the moral reforms of the age. There are partial exceptions, yet not enough to render the fact otherwise than general. We have also another corroborated fact: the almost universal absence of revival influence in the churches. The spiritual apathy is almost all-pervading, and is fearfully deep; so the religious press of the whole land testifies. Very extensively, church members are becoming devotees of fashion—joining hands with the ungodly in parties of pleasure, in dancing, in festivities, etc.

But we need not expand this painful subject. Suffice it that the evidence thickens and rolls heavily upon us, to show that the *churches generally are becoming sadly degenerate.* They have gone very far from the Lord, and he has withdrawn himself from them."

It may be said that our views of the moral fall and spiritual dearth of the churches are sh·wn to be incorrect by the great revivals of 1858. Of the fruit of these revivals let the leading Congregational and Baptist papers of Boston bear testimony.

Says the *Congregationalist* for Nov., 1858: "The revival piety of our churches is not such that one can confidently infer, from its mere existence, its legitimate, practical fruits. It ought, for example, to be as certain, after such a shower of grace, that the treasuries of our benevolent societies would be filled, as it is after a plentiful rain that the streams will swell in their channels. But the managers of our societies are bewailing the feebleness of the sympathy and aid of the churches.

"There is another and sadder illustration of the same general truth. The *Watchman and Reflector* recently stated that there had never been, among the Baptists, so lamentable a spread of church dissension as prevails at present. And the sad fact is mentioned that this sin infects the very churches which shared most largely in the late revival. And the still more melancholy fact is added, that these alienations date back their origin, in most cases, to the very midst of that scene of awakening. Even a glance at the weekly journals of our own denomination will evince that the evil is by no means confined to the

Baptists. Our own columns have, perhaps, never borne so humiliating a record of contentions and ecclesiastical litigations as during the last few months."

A Presbyterian pastor, of Belfast, Ireland (1858), uses the following language respecting the recent revivals in this country: " The determination to crush all ministers who say a word against their national sin [slavery], the determination to suffocate and suppress the plain teachings of Scripture, can be persisted in and carried out at the very time these New York Christians are expecting the religious world to hail their revivals. Until the wretchedly degraded churches of America do the work of God in their own land,' they have no spiritual vitality to communicate to others; their revivals are in the religious world what their flaunted cries of liberty, intermingled with the groans of the slave, are in the political."*

During the time of the great Irish revival of 1859, the General Assembly of the Presbyterian Church of Ireland held its session in Belfast. Says the Belfast *News-Letter*, of Sept. 30: "Here in this venerable body of ministers and elders, we find two ministers openly giving each other the lie, and the whole General Assembly turned into a scene of confusion bordering upon a riot."

These sad facts need no comment. In Ireland the ministers of the gospel are unable to meet in General Assembly without a riot among themselves; in America, prayers for the enslaved were not allowed in the revival meetings. No wonder that fruit of genuine piety is difficult to be found.

---

* N. Y. *Independent*, Dec., 1859.

How unlike what God designed that his people should be, has this great city become! The church of Christ was to be the light of the world, a city set upon a hill, which could not be hid. Matt. 5:14–17. But instead of this, his professed people have united with the world, and joined in affinity with it. This unlawful union of the church and the world (James 4:4) has resulted in her rejection by God; for how can the God of truth and holiness recognize as his people those who, in addition to their departure from their Lord, have rejected with scorn the tidings of his speedy coming?

In Rev. 18 the message announcing the fall of Babylon is presented again, with additions, showing, as we understand, that there is in the future a mighty movement to take place on this subject. We have no doubt that God has many dear saints united with the various bodies of professed Christians. Those, we believe, will yet hear the call given in Rev. 18:4. There is, however, one important fact which demonstrates that it was the providence of God which caused the proclamation of the first and second angels' messages within a few years past. Rev. 14:6–8. Chap. 18, in presenting again the message respecting the fall of Babylon, informs us that she has become the hold of foul spirits, and a cage of every unclean and hateful bird. As a demonstration that we are correct in regard to the application of Rev. 14, let the present movement respecting the spirits of the dead answer. An innumerable host of demons are spreading themselves over the whole country, flooding the churches and religious bodies of the land to a very great extent. The immortality of the soul, a doctrine which is held by almost every church in the world, is the basis and foundation of all their work.   This extraordinary movement clearly evinces the rapid approach of the hour of temptation that shall come on all the world, to try them that dwell on the earth.

It is an interesting fact that the judgment on the great harlot, which is so fully described in Rev. 18, is shown to John by one of the seven angels having the seven vials filled with the wrath of God.   Rev. 17: 1.   From chap. 16: 17–21, we learn that the judgment on the harlot Babylon is inflicted by the angel having the seventh vial. Hence we may justly conclude that the angel who shows John the judgment of Babylon, is that one of the seven who has her judgment to inflict; in other words, it is the angel who has the seventh vial.   It is agreed on all hands that the seventh angel of Rev. 16 is yet future.   It follows, therefore, that Rev. 18, which describes the judgment on Babylon and gives the call to come out of her, belongs to the future.   It is manifest that Babylon is rapidly becoming the hold of foul spirits, and of unclean and hateful birds.   The call to come out of her is made while her plagues are immediately impending.

The destruction of Babylon, as described in Rev. 18, takes place under the seventh vial; for it is under that vial that she comes in remembrance before God, to give unto her the cup of the wine of the fierceness of his wrath.   Rev. 16: 17–21.   The people of God are called out of her just before the seven last plagues are poured out. Those plagues are future, as we shall hereafter prove.   Hence it is certain that Rev. 18 cannot be applied to the events of the sixteenth century. It is manifest that the destruction of Babylon be-

gins before the great battle takes place; for the
kings are spared to witness her destruction (Rev.
18); but in the great battle they are all destroyed.
Rev. 19. While the saints eat the marriage supper, they behold the smoke of her burning; and
in response to the call of Rev. 18: 20, they rejoice
over her. Rev. 19: 1–9.

Babylon is to be thrown down with violence,
as a millstone is cast into the great deep, and she
is to be utterly burned with fire. If this utter
destruction were her "fall," there would be no
need of the second angel's proclamation to announce the fact; for her destruction is to be witnessed by the kings and merchants, and by every
ship-master, and by all the company in ships, and
by sailors, and by as many as trade by sea. This
is conclusive proof that the fall and destruction
of Babylon are not the same, and that Babylon itself is not a literal city; for its destruction causes
results that the destruction of no city on the
globe could cause. It is evident from what has
been said, that the destruction of Babylon takes
place in immediate connection with the second
advent. This fact is of itself a sufficient refuta-
tion of the view that locates the call, "Come out
of her, my people," in the future age; for Babylon
is destroyed at the very commencement of that
age.

The duty of the people of God is plainly expressed, "Come out of her, my people, that ye be
not partakers of her sins, and that ye receive not
of her plagues." Her sins have reached unto
heaven, and God has remembered her iniquities;
she has united herself to the kings of earth, and
confided in the arm of flesh, and not in Jehovah.
For the sake of this protection, she has smoothed

down the terrible threatenings of God's word against sin, and has thrown the mantle of religion over some of the basest of human crimes. As an instance, we will cite the Fugitive Slave Law, which during its existence had the sanction of many of the leading doctors of divinity. Pride, love of the world, and departure from God too plainly identify the Babylon of the Apocalypse with St. Paul's description of the popular church of the last days. 2 Tim. 3: 1–5. "From such," says the apostle, "turn away." If we would not partake of her sins, and thus share in the plagues that are about to be poured out upon her, we must heed the voice from heaven, "Come out of her, my people."

The moral fall of the Protestant churches in general brings us to the point where we are able to say, in the language of the Second Angel's Message, "Babylon is fallen, is fallen, that great city." This was not true of all Babylon before this moral fall had been witnessed, and consequently the second message would not have been appropriate if it had been preached before 1844. Only two divisions of Babylon had fallen before this time.

The Bible presents a testimony of the most solemn character concerning Babylon. It must be the duty of God's servants to give this testimony at the proper time, even as God has given it in his word. This testimony comes from God, and is not dependent upon the will of man, and therefore no person should be offended when it is presented. If that which is said of Babylon is true of a particular denomination, then that people should receive the light with gratitude, and bring forth the fruits of repentance. But if any church is found to whom this testimony is not applicable, let them be grateful that they do not belong to this great city, and let them not complain that this most solemn message is preached for the benefit of the vast numbers for whom it is appropriate. The servants of God are called to announce the principles of truth with faithfulness, and each one must apply them in his own case according to truth in the fear of God.

Now, lest any should deny that the Greek and the Protestant churches are included in Babylon, we invite attention to the following facts: It is evident, from the terms of this prophecy, that Babylon is composed of people who profess to be Christians. It is also evident that a great part of the true people of God are found in Babylon, even in the last days. But Babylon is a harlot because of her unlawful union with the kings of the earth; and as the result of this union she has corrupted the truth of God. Now we will prove that the Greek Church is one of the three grand divisions of Babylon. The Catholic Church became a harlot at an epoch at least as early as the time of Constantine. History records the acts of no other civil ruler who has wrought so great changes in the church as did Constantine. He gave a new form of government to the church, having for his model the government of the empire. He created offices in the church unknown to the New Testament, and he corrupted the doctrines and practices of the church. In his time the Greek Church and the Roman Church formed together the one so-called Catholic Church.

This great church continued to corrupt itself more and more from century to century. Its history is full of examples of unlawful union with the kings of the earth. But in the eleventh century, as the result of the long quarrel between the bishop of Rome and the bishop of Constantinople concerning the supremacy, the Catholic Church was divided into two churches, the Roman Catholic Church, and the Greek Catholic Church. After this separation, the Greek Catholic Church continued to be what the general Catholic Church had been before the division. The separation did not cause the Greek Church to renounce a single error of the great Catholic Church, nor to cease her unlawful connection with the kings of the earth. If the Catholic Church was Babylon before it was thus divided, then the Greek Church was, before that separation from Rome, a very considerable part of the great city Babylon. The principal difference between the Roman Church and the Greek Church since the separation is, that the Greek Church has simply retained the errors held by all in common before the separation, without making much addition to those errors, and without taking a very active part in persecuting others; while the Roman Church has added several other errors to her system of doctrine, particularly such as have respect to the power of the pope, and she has been very active in persecuting those who have not submitted to her authority. The Greek Church is less guilty than the church of Rome; but to deny that she forms an important division of Babylon, would be to deny that Babylon existed before the great schism of the eleventh century.

Five hundred years after the separation of the Greek and Roman churches bring us to the Reformation of the sixteenth century, which sepa-

rated several great nations from the communion
of the church of Rome. This is the second grand
separation from Rome. Since that time, the religious world has existed in three grand divisions,
the Greek Catholics, the Roman Catholics, and
the Protestants. The separation of the Greeks
from Rome was not characterized by a reformation; it is therefore certain that the Greeks continued to be a part of Babylon. But the separation of the Protestants from Rome was characterized by the renunciation of several great errors. It
is therefore worthy of our attention to determine
carefully whether the Protestants made such a
reform as would cause them to cease to be a part
of Babylon. They rejected the authority of the
pope and of the church of Rome; they appealed
to the Bible as the supreme rule of faith; they
exposed many errors and sins of the church of
Rome; and they taught justification by faith.

But to leave Babylon it is not enough to separate from the communion of those who sustain
her errors. It is necessary to renounce these errors by receiving the truth of God, and it is necessary, also, to renounce the sins of Babylon by
true repentance. If the Protestants returned to
the purity and simplicity of the New Testament,
then they ceased to be a part of Babylon; but if
they retained a considerable number of the essential errors and sins of Babylon, and contented
themselves to preserve their part of the old city,
after a partial purification, instead of building
anew after the divine model, then they have never
ceased to be a part of Babylon. The churches of
the New Testament were composed of those only
who repented of their sins, believed on the Lord
Jesus Christ, and were buried with him in bap-

tism. But the churches which compose the Romish apostasy are organized on a plan essentially different from that of the apostles. By means of infant baptism, the entire population is brought into the church; the church and the world are no longer distinct, and the church becomes an assembly of unconverted men. This confusion of the world and the church is one of the essential errors which made a Babylon of the Catholic church. Now it is a painful fact that the reformers did not see it necessary to commence at the foundation, and form churches of converted persons only on the contrary, they positively refused to do this, and they not only retained infant baptism, but their first churches were simply Romish churches which had accepted the doctrines of the Reformation, but which were composed of persons admitted by infant baptism, the larger part of whom were unacquainted with Christian experience; and the churches afterward raised up by them were of a similar character, because formed on the same model.

Now we offer a second decisive proof that the Reformation was not sufficiently complete to deliver the Protestants from Babylon. The unlawful union of Church and State is the natural consequence of the prevalence of infant baptism; for that human ordinance made the terms *church* and *world* two names for one thing. This shows how appropriate is the term *Babylon* as the name for this city of confusion. But Babylon is called a prostitute because of her unlawful union with the kings of the earth. This criminal union is seen when by their royal authority they exercise their influence in forming the doctrines of the church, in giving form to the service and worship of God,

and in creating offices in the church, and filling
them with their favorites; and when the church
not only accepts all this, but even sanctions the
criminal practices of kings, so that she may profit
by their revenues, and that she may use this power
to persecute those who do not accept her dogmas.
Was it true that the reformers separated Church
and State in Germany, Switzerland, Denmark,
Sweden, Norway, Scotland, and England? Did
they imitate the apostles in organizing churches
without the participation of the civil power?—By
no means. In all these countries the civil power
has exercised a strong influence in the formation
of the confessions of faith, and in deciding what
should be the character and manner of the worship, in creating church offices, and in selecting
the persons to fill those offices, and even in deter-
mining who should be the ministers of the word
of God. These things are carried so far in England that the king or queen is recognized as the
head of the church. This unlawful union of
Church and State made Babylon a prostitute, and
the reformers did not dissolve this union, but perpetuated it.

The ordinances of the church have been corrupted in Babylon. To leave Babylon it is necessary to turn from these corruptions, and to receive the pure ordinances of the New Testament
church. Did the reformers see the necessity of
doing this?—They did not. They were satisfied
with the baptism they had received in their in-
fancy from the Catholic priests, and they perpetuated this corruption of the ordinance of baptism
in the Protestant churches. They served in the
work of the Christian ministry by virtue of their
ordination as Catholic priests, and they never con-

sidered it important to be set apart to the holy ministry by converted men. They were satisfied with that which they had received from Rome. Even the bishops and archbishops of the ancient Catholic Church of England have been perpetuated in the Church of England and in the Episcopal Church of America, and these churches pretend to be the Catholic Church, or rather, grand divisions of that church, because they can trace their bishops back to the apostles through the long line of popes.

These things show that the Reformation formed the third grand division of Babylon, instead of establishing a church upon the model of the ancient apostolic church. This third division is much less soiled with error than are the other two divisions, but it is not clean in the sight of God. Since the Reformation, other Protestant churches have arisen, having less of papal errors than the first reformed churches. But a serious error which is at the foundation of the great Babylonian apostasy is found in nearly all the Protestant churches. That great apostasy has virtually annulled the commandment which forbids graven images, and the commandment which commands men to sanctify the seventh day in memory of the Creator's rest. The action of the church of Rome with respect to the first of these commandments was considered by the reformers a just ground for separation from that church, and yet nearly all the Protestant churches have perpetuated the action of that great apostasy with respect to the fourth commandment. They violate the fourth commandment, and teach men so; or rather, they make void the commandment of God to keep the tradition of the elders. They set aside the Sabbath of the Lord that they may keep the festival day of the sun; and in thus violating the fourth commandment, they actually violate the entire law of God. No church has a right to consider itself apostolic while it violates the commandments of God. So long as a church does this, the stain of apostasy is upon her, and in this respect she is Babylonian rather than apostolic.

Though the account of the judgment upon Babylon in Rev. 18 speaks of Babylon as if she were one city, yet we learn from Rev. 16:19 that Babylon will be divided into three parts before she receives her punishment. This seems to indicate that these three parts are not alike guilty, and that God makes this division that he may punish each part according to the light which it has had, and the crimes which it has committed. It is therefore not unreasonable to conclude that Babylon is now composed of three grand sections, which are culpable in different degrees, and that God will judge each according to its deserts. The Roman Catholic Church, having its seat at Rome, and having once had the jurisdiction of the entire ten kingdoms, and now of the greater part of them, is without doubt the central section of this great city; but we have convincing proof that there are also two other sections of Babylon, and that God will punish each as it deserves.

The fall of this great city is announced after the third and last section has fallen. It is only then we are able to say in truth that Babylon is fallen. The place assigned to this proclamation in prophecy is the only place suitable for it. For us to be able to leave Babylon, it is necessary that the angel of God should illuminate the earth with his glory (Rev. 18:1, 2), and thus dissipate the darkness which its errors have caused. This angel accomplishes his work in intimate connection with the angel who announces that the hour of God's Judgment is come, and with that other angel who preaches the commandments of God and the faith of Jesus. It is at the time of these messages that the people of God are called out of Babylon,—a proof conclusive that the greater part are in Babylon when this proclamation is made. The coming of Christ must be preceded by a work which shall establish the primitive purity, and this work must be accomplished by the three angels. Consequently, the proclamation concerning Babylon pertains to the end of this dispensation.

CHAPTER V.

THE PROCLAMATION OF THE THIRD ANGEL.

This Proclamation not a Past Event—It Relates to the Work of the Two-Horned Beast—The Ten-Horned Beast—Its Identity with the Little Horn of Dan. 7—The Seven Heads—The Ten Horns—The Deadly Wound—The Mouth Speaking Great Things—Fate of the Beast.

"And the third angel followed them, saying with a loud voice, If any man worship the beast and his image, and receive his mark in his forehead, or in his hand, the same shall drink of the wine of the wrath of God, which is poured out without mixture into the cup of his indignation; and he shall be tormented with fire and brimstone in the presence of the holy angels, and in the presence of the Lamb: and the smoke of their torment ascendeth up forever and ever; and they have no rest day nor night, who worship the beast and his image, and whosoever receiveth the mark of his name. Here is the patience of the saints; here are they that keep the commandments of God, and the faith of Jesus." Verses 9–12.

THIS is the most solemn warning that the Bible contains. As the pen of inspiration has recorded this language for our instruction, it will be wise for us to listen and obey. It is certain that the record of our world's history presents no testimony that this message has been heard in the past. And the fact that the first and second angels of this series have been proved to belong to the present generation, most clearly establishes the point that this message does not belong to past ages.

Says J. V. Himes, in 1847: "But the fourteenth chapter [of Revelation] presents an astounding cry, *yet to be made*, as a warning to mankind in that hour of strong temptation. Verses 9–11. A denunciation of wrath so dreadful cannot be found in the book of God, besides this. Does it not imply a strong temptation, to require so terrific an admonition?"*

The work of the two-horned beast in performing miracles, and causing those that dwell upon the earth, by means of those miracles, to form an image to the beast which all men must worship, certainly pertains to the future. The Third Angel's Message is a warning to prepare the church for this fearful scene. In proof of this fact, we place the prophecy respecting the two-horned beast, and the warning of the third angel, in contrast:—

Of the two-horned beast the prophet says: "And he exerciseth all the power of the first beast before him, and causeth the earth and them which dwell therein to worship the first beast, whose deadly wound was healed. . . . And he had power to give life unto the image of the beast, that the image of the beast should both speak, and cause that as many as would not worship the image of the beast should be killed. And he causeth all, both small and great, rich and poor, free and bond, to receive a mark in their right hand, or in their foreheads; and that no man might buy or sell, save he that had the mark, or the name of the beast, or the number of his name." Chap. 13:12–17.

---

* "Facts on Romanism," p. 112.

Of the warning of the third angel he says: "If any man worship the beast and his image, and receive his mark in his forehead, or in his hand, the same shall drink of the wine of the wrath of God, which is poured out without mixture into the cup of his indignation; and he shall be tormented with fire and brimstone in the presence of the holy angels, and in the presence of the Lamb; and the smoke of their torment ascendeth up forever and ever; and they have no rest day nor night, who worship the beast and his image, and whosoever receiveth,the mark of his name." Rev. 14: 9–11.

A comparison of these scriptures shows us what an hour of temptation and anguish there is yet before us. If men worship the beast and his image, they will receive of the wine of the wrath of God; and if they refuse, it is at the peril of their lives at the hands of men. This doubtless refers to the time when all who dwell upon the earth, whose names are not written in the book of life, shall worship the beast. Rev. 13: 8.

That we may understand the cause of this fearful warning against the worship of the beast and his image, and the reception of his mark, it is necessary that we should examine the testimony respecting the beast, and also the two-horned beast that causes the image to be made to the first beast. What, then, is the beast ?

This question may be answered by referring to Rev. 13: 1–10. When Daniel, in his vision of the seventh chapter, was shown the various empires that should successively bear rule over the earth, they were represented under the symbols of beasts arising from the sea. Three of these having passed away in John's day, it is proper that the fourth of this series, only, should be shown to him. The beast with ten horns, described by Daniel, is also seen by John to ascend out of the sea.

In him were blended the marks of all the preceding beasts,—the body of the leopard, the feet of the bear, and the mouth of the lion. Dan. 7 : 4–6. The beast is evidently the papal form of the fourth empire; for it receives its power and seat from the dragon, imperial Rome. Verse 2. In proof of this, we present the following evidence as arranged by Litch. He is showing the identity of the papal power in Dan. 7 with the beast of Rev. 13 : 1–10.

"1. The little horn was to be a blasphemous power. 'He shall speak great words against the Most High.' Dan. 7 : 25. So, also, was the beast of Rev. 13 : 6 to do the same. 'He opened his mouth in blasphemy againt God.'

"2. The little horn 'made war with the saints, and prevailed against them.' Dan. 7 : 21. Thus the beast of Rev. 13 : 7 was also 'to make war with the saints, and to overcome them.'

"3. The little horn had a 'mouth that spake very great things.' Dan. 7 : 8, 20. So, likewise, there was given the beast of Rev. 13 : 5 'a mouth speaking great things and blasphemies.'

"4. Power was given the little horn of Dan. 7 : 25, 'until a time, times, and the dividing of time.' To the beast, also, power was given to 'continue forty and two months.' Rev. 13 : 5.

" 5. The dominion of the little horn was to be
taken away at the termination of that specified
period. The beast of Rev. 13 : 10, who led into
captivity and put to death with the sword so
many of the saints, was himself to be led into
captivity, and be killed with the sword, at the
end of the forty and two months.

" With these points of similarity in the two
emblems, the little horn and the beast, who can
doubt their identity ?*

"The dragon (imperial Rome) gave unto the
beast (papal Rome) his power, and his seat, and
great authority."

We have, before proved that the city of Rome
was the seat of the dragon, which is here represented as transferred to the beast. It is well
known that the seat of empire was by the emperor
Constantine removed from Rome to Constantinople ; and that Rome itself, at a later period,
was given to the popes by the Emperor Justinian.

The seven heads are seven forms of civil power
which successively bear rule. These seven heads
belong alike to the dragon of Rev. 12, the beast
of chap. 13, and that of chap. 17. This shows
conclusively that the dragon and these two
beasts are symbols of the same power under
different heads ; for there are not three sets of
seven heads, but it is evident that the heads are
successive forms of its power, one of them bearing rule at a time, and then giving place to another. Rev. 17 : 9, 10. It appears that the
dragon of chap. 12 and the beast of chap. 13 and
that of chap. 17 each represents some one or
more of the seven heads ; yet as each is seen with

* "Restitution," pp. 119, 120.

the seven heads, they must each in a certain sense extend over all the period covered by the three symbols ; for there are not twenty-one heads. The proper period of each seems to be this : the dragon before the 1260 years, the beast of chap. 13 during that period, and the beast of chap. 17 since the deadly wound and captivity at the close of that period.

The ten horns are the ten kingdoms of the fourth empire.   They are distinct from the seven heads, and hence the ten kingdoms are not to be counted as one of the heads as some have done. The horns are contemporary, that is, all reign at the same time ; while the heads are successive, but one existing at a time.   It seems that John, in Rev. 13: 1–10, goes twice over the history of the beast, once in verses 1–3, and again in verses 4–10.   We now inquire respecting the time when the beast received its deadly wound.   That this event took place at the close of the 1260 years, and not before the commencement of that period, or during its continuance, we think evident from the following facts:—

1. A head wounded before that period would not be a head of the beast, but a head of the dragon.   The prophecy does not relate to the wounding of a head of the dragon, to make way for the rise of the beast, as some suppose, but to the wounding of a head of the beast.

2. Nor could it take place during the 1260 years; for it is said that the beast receives his power and seat from this dragon, and that from that time he was to have power for 1260 years, so that he should be able to overcome the saints, and should have power over all kindreds and tongues and nations.   This 1260 years' rule be-

gan with the act of the dragon in giving his seat, the city of Rome, unto the beast, in 538, and ended in 1798, when the city of Rome was taken from the beast, and his power was wrested from him. During this period, therefore, the deadly wound and overthrow of the beast could not take place.

3. The time when the beast received this deadly wound seems to be clearly marked in verse 10. It is there stated that he that leadeth into captivity and killeth with the sword, must be led into captivity and killed with the sword. That is, the papal power, which had thus acted for 1260 years, must at the close of that period of triumph be thus used. Such were the facts in 1798. So John goes over the history of the beast twice, first in verses 1–3, ending with the deadly wound ; and the second time in verses 4–10, ending with the beast's being led into captivity and slain. This is the event predicted in Dan. 7 : 26 : "They shall take away his dominion."

The mouth given to the beast speaking great words and blasphemies, evidently signifies the same as the mouth of the little horn of Dan. 7, which should speak great words against the Most High, and think to change times and laws. It is the papacy claiming infallibility, and pretending to be the vicar of God upon earth. That this prophecy has been fulfilled in the most wonderful manner, and that the 1260 years of papal triumph expired about the close of the last century, cannot be denied. The papal power was then subverted, and the seat of the dragon wrested from him. We believe, however, that verse 8— " And all that dwell upon the earth shall worship him, whose names are not written in the book of life of the Lamb slain from the foundation of the world "—has never yet been fully accomplished. It is certain that the time never yet has been when *all* except true Christians worshiped the beast.   But this time is yet to be witnessed in the fulfillment of the prophecy respecting the two-horned beast.   We expect this in the hour of temptation that shall come on all the world, to try them that dwell upon the earth.   It is in view of this scene that the third angel utters his voice of warning.   The beast of Rev. 13 : 1–10, though wounded with a deadly wound, was to recover from that wound, and must, according to Rev. 19 : 19, 20 and Dan. 7 : 7–11, continue till the battle of the great day of God Almighty, after which he is to be cast into the lake of fire.

———•———

CHAPTER VI.

THE TWO-HORNED BEAST.

The Two-horned Beast cannot arise in the Ten Kingdoms of Papal Europe—Time and Manner of his Rise—Testimony of the Dublin *Nation*—Symbol of the Two Horns—The Dragon Voice—An Age of Wonders—The Spirits of Devils working Miracles—The Hour of Temptation.

It is the two-horned beast that is to cause the world to worship the first beast, and to form an image to that beast, which all must worship on pain of death.   We have shown that it is the two-horned beast which is to cause the fearful scene respecting which the third angel utters his voice of solemn warning. It is therefore evident that if we would understand this warning, we must carefully examine the prophecy respecting the two-horned beast. What power, then, is symbolized by this beast with two horns like a lamb? We have already seen that the fourth beast of Daniel, which in its papal form is the same as the beast that received the deadly wound, of which John speaks, does not give his place to another beast, but continues until the Judgment, when he is to be cast into the fiery flame. Dan. 7 : 11 ; Rev. 19 : 20. Hence it is certain that the *location* of the two-horned beast is not in the ten kingdoms of the fourth beast. We cannot take one of the horns of the fourth beast, and with it constitute another beast, or the horns of another.

The two-horned beast is "another beast" besides the ten-horned beast. It is not the first beast healed of his deadly wound ; for the work of the two-horned beast is in the sight of that beast. Rev. 13 : 14. It would indeed be a surprising change if the ten horns were to be plucked up, and in their stead two other horns should arise. Yet such is a necessary conclusion if the two-horned beast is but another form of the first beast. Hence we conclude that the two-horned beast is another and a distinct power.

It is, however, from the time of its rise a power *contemporary* with the beast whose deadly wound was healed. It acts in the sight of the first beast in performing its wonders.

The *manner* of its rise is not to be overlooked. The four beasts of Daniel, of which series John's first beast constituted the fourth, are all seen to rise out of the sea in consequence of the striving of the winds. Dan. 7 : 2, 3 ; Rev. 13 : 1. They arose by overturning the powers that preceded them, by means of general war. Winds denote war or strife among men, and sea or waters denote people, nations, etc. Rev. 7 : 1–3 ; 17 : 15. But this power arises in a peaceful or lamb-like manner from the earth. It does not arise by the strife of the winds upon the sea, that is, by the overthrow of other nations and empires, but it arises where no other beast exists, and acts its part in the presence of its predecessors. This shows that it must arise from a new and previously unoccupied territory.

When was this power to arise ?—Not prior to the *first* beast, certainly. Not at the same time; for then there would be no propriety in designating either as the first beast It is said that it shall exercise all the power of the first beast before it. Then we may look for it to come on the stage of action about the close of the first beast's dominion, at the end of the 1260 years. Again, it is to cause the world to worship the first beast, whose deadly wound was healed, which shows that its period of action is this side of 1798.

J. Litch says : "The two-horned beast is represented as a power existing and performing his part after the death and revival of the first beast. . . . If asked for my opinion as to what will constitute that beast with two horns, or the false prophet, I must frankly confess I do not know. I think it is a power yet to be developed or made manifest as an accomplice of the papacy in subjecting the world. It will be a power which will perform miracles, and deceive the world with them. See Rev. 19 : 20."*

---

* "Restitution," pp. 131, 133.

Mr. Wesley, in his notes on Rev. 13, says of the two-horned beast: "He has not yet come, though he cannot be far off; for he is to appear at the end of the forty-two months of the first beast."

One fact of interest may be noticed here : The course of empire, beginning with the first great empire near the garden of Eden, has been ever tending westward. Thus the seat of the Babylonian and Persian empires was in Asia. The seat of the Grecian and Roman empires was in Europe. The Roman Empire, in its divided state, as represented by the ten horns, occupies all the remaining territory west of the Atlantic Ocean. Hence, we still look westward for the rise of the power described in this prophecy.

Bishop Berkeley, in his celebrated poem on America, written before the American Revolution, foresaw the greatness of this power, and he forcibly describes its connection with its predecessors:—

> "Westward the course of empire takes its way;
>   The first four acts already past,
> A fifth shall end the drama with the day;
>   Time's noblest offspring is the last."

By "the four acts" the bishop doubtless refers to the four great empires of the prophet Daniel. The fifth, with which the scene closes, is the power that has arisen this side of the Atlantic. As the four powers of the Eastern Continent were not to be succeeded by a fifth, we understand that the power represented by the beast with two horns, which arises in the last days of the fourth beast, must be located in America. This lamb-like power, the noblest and the last offspring of time, must also in its dragonic character prove itself the basest. As we have said, the two-horned beast does not arise by overthrowing its predecessors. And it is worthy of notice that the ten kingdoms of the fourth empire were all complete long before the discovery of America. The war of the Revolution was not for the purpose of overthrowing one of the ten kingdoms of the fourth empire, but it was to maintain the just rights of the American people.

This power is evidently the last one with which the people of God are connected; for the Third Angel's Message, which immediately precedes the coming of Jesus on the white cloud, pertains almost entirely to the action of the two-horned beast. Compare Rev. 14:9-11 with 13:11-18. And it is a fact which ought not to be overlooked, that those powers with which the people of God are connected, are the only ones noted in prophecy. It is also plain that the march of civilization and of Christianity, like the course of the natural sun, has ever been westward; and it is evident that the territory of this last power is to be the field of the angels' messages, the land where the crowning truths of the gospel, as it finishes its course, are to be brought out.

The rise of each of the great powers has been gradual. For a series of years they were preparing for the stations which they afterward assumed; but they begin to be represented in prophecy *at the time when they are prepared to act their part.* We are now to trace the rise of an empire which has come up in the sight of the first beast,—a power still further on toward the setting sun, with the history of which the great circuit of empire will be accomplished, for the boundary of the vast Pacific has been reached.

A short time before the Reformation in the days of Martin Luther, a new continent was discovered. The rise of the reformers brought out a large class who were determined to worship God according to the dictates of their own conscience. They desired a greater measure of civil and religious freedom; hence they with many others fled to the wilds of America, and laid the foundation of a new empire. They did not establish their power by overturning another power, but they planted themselves in an uncultivated waste, and laid the foundation of a new government. The preceding powers had arisen through the strife of the winds on the great sea; but this power arises out of the earth. That is, the first powers arose through the action of wars in overturning and subverting other nations, to be in turn overthrown and subverted by their successors; but this power appears to arise from the earth in a peaceful manner. It comes up in the sight of the first beast like the settlement and growth of a new country.

The Dublin *Nation* thus notices the progress and the power of this republic: " In the East, there is arising a colossal centaur called the Russian Empire. With a civilized head and front, it has the sinews of a huge barbaric body. There one man's brain moves 70,000,000. There all the traditions of the people are of aggression and conquest in the West. There but two ranks are distinguishable, serfs and soldiers. There the map of the future includes Constantinople and Vienna as outposts of St. Petersburg.

"In the West, an opposing and still more wonderful American Empire is EMERGING. We islanders have no conception of the extraordinary events which, *amid the silence of the earth*, are daily adding to. the power and pride of this gigantic nation. Within three years, territories more extensive than these three kingdoms, France, and Italy put together, have been *quietly*, and in almost ' matter of course ' fashion, annexed to the Union.

" In seventy years, seventeen new sovereignties, the smallest of them larger than Great Britain, have peaceably united themselves to the federation. No standing army was raised, no national debt sunk, no great exertion was made, but there they are. And the last mail brings news of the organization of three more great States about to be joined to the thirty, Minnesota in the north-west, Deseret in the south-west, and California on the shores of the Pacific. These three States will cover an area equal to one-half the European continent.

" Nor is this a mere addition on the map. It is not piling barren Pelion upon uncultivated Ossa. It is an actual conquest of new strength and resources. Already has Minnesota its capital, St. Paul, which has its journals, churches, schools, parties, interests, and speculations. . . . Instead of becoming a lawless horde of adventurers, the settlers in California are founding cities, electing delegates, magistrates, sheriffs, and congressmen as methodically and as intently as if they trod the beaten paths of life on the Atlantic shore of the continent.

" And with this increase of territory, there is a commensurate increase of industry in the older States. The census of 1850, about to be taken in the United States, will show a growth of numbers, territory, and industry entirely unexampled in human history.   Let the 'gray powers of the Old World' look to it; let the statesmen of France, Germany, and Russia read the census carefully, though it should startle them.   Let despotism count every man of these millions as a mortal enemy, and every acre of that vast commonwealth as an inheritance of mankind mortgaged to the cause of freedom.   America is as grand a field for human enterprise as when the ships of Columbus first neared the shores of Guanahani."

The progress of our country since its first settlement has indeed been wonderful.   We trace its rise onward, from the time of its first settlement by those who fled from the oppression of the fourth empire till it assumes its station among the great powers of earth, a little previous to the end of the 1260 years.   Its territory has increased more than three-fold since that period, by the addition of the vast territories of Louisiana, Florida, Texas, New Mexico, and California, and the extension of an undisputed title to Oregon, thus extending its dominion to the vast Pacific.

The youth, as well as the *apparent* mildness of this power, seems to be indicated by its lamb-like horns.   What do these horns mean ?   The symbol of horns like those of a lamb is not elsewhere used in the prophetic scriptures, with the exception of those texts which represent Christ as a lamb having seven horns, etc.   Rev. 5: 6.   The idea appears to be generally prevalent, that a horn is used only to designate *civil* power.   This is certainly a mistake.

"The horn as an emblem of power was originally taken from beasts, such as the urus, wild ox, buffalo, or perhaps the rhinoceros, who were perceived to have so much power in their horns. Hence, a horn was frequently worn on crowns and helmets, as is evident on ancient coins ; and to this day it is an appendage to the diadems of the kings and chiefs of Abyssinia."

We may learn from those symbols, which are explained in connection with other powers, some facts that will throw light on this. The two horns of the ram in Dan. 8 denoted the union of the two powers of Media and Persia in one empire. The great horn of the Grecian goat was the symbol of the first *form* of that power. The ten horns of the fourth beast denoted the ten distinct powers into which the fourth empire was divided. Dan. 7: 23–25. And the little horn which came up after the ten, represented the papacy, *a purely ecclesiastical power*. It was a *horn* before the three were plucked up. See Dan. 7: 8, 24. This was accomplished in 538, but the papacy did not become possessed of temporal dominion until 755.

Says Goodrich: "As a reward to the Roman pontiff, Pepin, in the year 755, conferred on Stephen, the successor of Zachary, several rich provinces in Italy, by which gift he was established as a *temporal monarch*."*

Hence it is certain that *ecclesiastical* as well as civil power is represented by a horn. And it is evident that the horns of these beasts symbolize the entire power of the beasts. From these facts we may learn that the horns of Daniel's fourth beast (the first beast of Rev. 13) denoted civil and religious power. Hence we regard the horns

---

"History of the Church," p. 98; "Bowers's History of the Popes," vol. 2, p. 108.

of the last beast of Rev. 13 as symbolizing the civil and religious power of the nation represented by that beast. A plurality of horns is not always the symbol of a power *divided;* for the two horns of the ram in Dan. 8 symbolize the *union* of Media and Persia in one government. In appearance, if we may judge from the symbols used, this beast represents the mildest power that ever rose; for in the prophetic history of the governments that have preceded this, no one has been represented by symbols so mild. We understand these horns to denote the civil and religious power of this nation,—its Republican civil power, and its Protestant ecclesiastical. If it be objected that its civil power ought to be represented by the beast, rather than by a horn of the beast, we refer to one or two facts that will meet this point. The civil power of Grecia was represented by the great horn of the goat; and when that civil power was broken, the beast still continued to exist; and in the place of that one civil government arose four. And we may add, that when the dominion of the different beasts of Dan. 7 was taken away, their lives were prolonged for a season and a time. That is, the nations still lived, though their dominion was destroyed. Hence, we understand that the beasts denote the nations which constitute the different kingdoms, and the horns of the beast denote the civil and religious powers of the nations.

No civil power could ever compare with Republicanism in its lamb-like character. The grand principle recognized by this form of power is thus expressed: "That all men are created equal; that they are endowed by their Creator with certain inalienable rights; that among these are life, liberty, and the pursuit of happiness." Hence all should have a right to participate in making the laws, and in designating who shall execute them. Was there ever a development of civil power so lamb-like before? And what, in religious matters, can be compared with Protestantism? Its leading sentiment is the distinct recognition of the right of private judgment in matters of conscience. "The Bible is the only religion of Protestants." Was there ever in the religious world anything to equal this in its lamb-like professions?

The symbol of the beast with two horns like a lamb fitly represents this new power. Observe the combination of the lamb and the dragon. Both these symbols had been previously seen by John. There is an evident reference to them in this description of the beast with two horns. He had seen a Lamb with seven horns and a dragon with tens horns. Rev. 5:6; 12:3. The Lamb represents Jesus Christ in his office of King of kings. Rev. 17:14. The dragon represents the Roman power animated by Satan. Rev. 12. In fact, if we omit the heads and horns which represent that empire in its several forms, we shall find that the real dragon, or serpent, is Satan himself. Rev. 20:2, 3, 7. The kingdom of Christ and the kingdom of Satan are opposite in character. Christ's kingdom is one and indivisible; but the kingdom of Satan is full of confusion and division. For this reason the horns of the Lamb and the horns of the dragon, though alike symbolic, are by the Spirit of God interpreted very differently. The horns of the dragon are the same as the horns of the beast to whom the dragon gave his power. They are the ten kingdoms, into which the kingdom of the dragon

or beast has been divided. Rev. 17:12; Dan.
7:24. But the horns of the Lamb, who is King
of kings, are the seven spirits of God. Rev. 5:6.
The seven horns must therefore represent the
nature of Christ's dominion as King of kings,
and not that his kingdom should be divided; for
his title, King of kings, indicates not one kingdom broken up into many, but rather many united
in one; for the servants of Christ will be princes
under him (Matt. 19:28; Luke 22:30; Rev. 20:
4; 21:24); and he, as King over an undivided
kingdom, will wear many crowns. Rev. 19:12.

In the symbol of the two-horned beast, the
character of the horns, and *not merely the number,* is intended to be expressed by the words,
"two horns like a lamb"; for there is nothing
peculiar to a lamb with respect to the *number* of
its horns, but there is something peculiar in the
character of these horns. It is important to notice this fact ; for the interpretation of the horns
of a lamb in John's vision is essentially different
from that of the horns of the dragon, or of the
beast. Thus the horns of the beast represent the
division of his kingdom ; but the horns of the
lamb represent the *nature* of his power, and do
not signify that his kingdom is to be divided.
We therefore understand the two horns like those
of a lamb to represent the nature of the power
symbolized, and not that it should be divided
into two parts.

The Spirit of God, in giving us the symbol of
the ten-horned beast, thought proper to place
crowns upon each of those horns. But in giving
us the symbol of the beast with two horns like
those of a lamb, it placed no crowns upon those
horns. Now these two symbols are not only

given in immediate connection, but they are joined in the same work, according to this prophecy. Rev. 13:1, 11, 12, 14; 16:13; 19:20. It cannot, therefore, be without design that crowns are placed upon the horns of the first beast, and omitted in the case of the second. We know that the horns with crowns represent kingly governments (Rev. 17:12); and we think it a necessary conclusion that these horns like those of a lamb, and without crowns, represent a government in which the *people* bear rule.

In some form, two kinds of power everywhere exist. These are, the *civil* power, as seen in the *State;* and the *spiritual* power as seen in the *Church.* In almost every country these powers are blended together in *one,* and both are in the hands of the rulers, and not in those of the people. But the American Republic presents the first instance in the history of the world in which these two powers are *separated,* and *both* are reserved by the people in their own hands. It is a government *by* the people and *for* the people, and it acknowledges them as the fountain of all authority. Here we have a State without a king and a Church without a pope; and Church and State are separate. The civil power recognizes the equality of all men before the law; and the spiritual power acknowledges the right of every man to worship God according to his own convictions of what God requires. Here are the two horns like those of a lamb.

"And he spake like a dragon." With all these lamb-like appearances, the real spirit by which he is actuated is that of the dragon,—the Devil. "For out of the abundance of the heart the mouth speaketh." Matt. 12:34. What he is to speak we may notice hereafter. Rev. 13:14.

"And he exerciseth all the power of the first beast before him [or in his sight, as Whiting translates it], and causeth the earth and them that dwell therein to worship the first beast, whose deadly wound was healed." Here is conclusive proof that the two-horned beast is distinct from the ten-horned beast, and contemporary with it from the time that its deadly wound was healed, or about the commencement of the present century. This exercise of power will constitute the very scene of trouble and danger before us, respecting which the third angel utters his voice of warning, "If any man worship the beast," etc. The anguish of that period, when all the power of the first beast shall be exercised, may be learned from reading the history of the first beast. Rev. 13:5–7; Dan. 7:23–26. It is certain that since the 1260 years of triumph of the first beast, no power has exercised such oppression as that which is here predicted. Hence this has not been accomplished in the past; and the prophecy clearly shows us that this dragonic work is to proceed from a government the mildest in appearance that the world ever saw, its power being represented by "horns like a lamb"; so that from a power that has presented to the world the most extraordinary spectacle of civil and religious liberty, bitter and unrelenting persecution is yet to be experienced by the church. This important fact should be carefully considered.

The lamb-like character is first to be exhibited. This is to deceive the nations. Then the dragonic character—the real character of the beast—is to appear. For as the dragon gave power to the first beast, and thus prepared the papacy for its 1260 years of persecution, so the two-horned beast gives power to the image of the first beast, to act a part like that beast in warring upon the saints. The only civil government that has ever existed, exhibiting the lamb-like appearance of this symbol, is the United States, one of the articles of its Constitution containing these words: "Congress shall make no law respecting an establishment of religion, or prohibiting the free exercise thereof." As the lamb-like power of this beast, represented by its horns, is not in accordance with its dragonic character, as exhibited in its exercising all the power of the first beast, we think the conclusion a reasonable one, that its period of mildness and deception precedes that of its tyranny and oppression. We shall notice hereafter what this power does in causing the world to worship the first beast.

That we are living in an age of wonders is an admitted fact. The expression is ofttimes repeated, "There is nothing too wonderful to happen." The increase of knowledge in every department of the arts and sciences has indeed been without precedent in our world's history. Our own country takes the lead in all this: we see the chariots, with the speed of lightning, coursing their way through the land, and with similar speed men traverse the mighty deep. The prophecy of Nahum is now literally fulfilled: "The chariots shall be with flaming torches in the day of His preparation, and the fir-trees shall be terribly shaken. The chariots shall rage in the streets, they shall justle one against another in the broad ways: they shall seem like torches, they shall run like the lightnings." Chap. 2:3, 4. "The fire of God" (the lightning, Job 1:16; Ex. 9:23, 24) has been here brought down from heaven. Such is the wonderful power that man has obtained over the elements. And the lightning thus brought down from heaven is now made obedient to the will of man, and sent as a messenger from one end of our land to the other. God said to Job, "Canst thou send lightnings, that they may go and say unto thee, Here we are?" Job 38:35. To send the lightning seems almost an attribute of Omnipotence, if we may judge from the manner in which Jehovah speaks to his ancient servant; yet men are now able to employ this executor of the wrath of God as their own obedient servant. It has been observed by one speaker: "If Franklin tamed the lightning, Prof. Morse taught it the English language." And all this bids fair to be eclipsed by other and more astonishing wonders.

We do not indeed regard this as the fulfillment of the prophecy, "He doeth great wonders, so that he maketh fire to come down from heaven on the earth in the sight of men;" but these facts are worthy of notice as marking the age in which we live. When men in ancient times had reached that pass that there was nothing restrained from them that they imagined to do, we read that God came down and confounded them. Gen. 11:6-9. If the men of the present generation do not occupy a similar position, they certainly bid fair to do so before long. The world may indeed be deceived by the things that we have named, and many others of a like character, and be caused to believe that better days are coming, and that the earth is being prepared for the happy residence of men, and that men are becoming more virtuous and enlightened, and that thus the way is preparing for the temporal millennium. But there is a class of wonders now in process of development that bids fair to present to the world the perfect fulfillment of this prophecy. We refer to that which is now called "Spiritualism," the work of the unclean spirits in our land.

In almost every part of our land, multitudes of men of every class are now holding communion, as they suppose, with the spirits of the dead. And that they are holding communion with spirits of some kind is undeniable, for the fact of their presence is attested by astounding miracles. We think that no one can deny the facts that are brought to substantiate the work of the spirits, however they may judge of·the spirits themselves.

Hon. J. W. Edmonds, judge of the Supreme Court of New York, said in 1853: "Scarcely more than four years have elapsed since the 'Rochester knockings' were first known among us. Then, mediums could be counted by units, but now, by thousands; then, believers could be numbered by the hundreds, now, by tens of thousands. It is believed by the best informed that the whole number in the United States must be several hundred thousand, and that in this city [New York] and its vicinity there must be from twenty to twenty-five thousand. There are ten or twelve newspapers and periodicals devoted to the cause, and the Spiritual library embraces more than one hundred different publications, some of which have already attained a circulation of more than ten thousand copies. Besides the undistinguished multitude, there are many men of high standing and talent ranked among them, —doctors, lawyers, and clergymen in great numbers, a Protestant bishop, the learned and reverend president of a college, judges of our higher courts, members of Congress, foreign embassadors, and ex-members of the United States Senate."

This statement of Judge Edmonds was written about 1855. Since that time this work of the spirits has been steadily progressing, and they have now extended themselves over Great Britain, France, Germany, and many other countries. The Roman pontiff, the Queen of Spain, and the Empress of France, also the late Emperor, have all sought to these spirits for knowledge. It may be proper that we enumerate some of the many remarkable acts performed by them. Among them are the following:—

Many well-attested cases of healing; writing performed by them without the aid of any one; the transportation of things from a distance by the spirits alone; and persons carried by the spirits through the air in the presence of many others. Tables have been suspended in the air with several persons on them; beautiful music has been performed by the spirits, with and without the aid of instruments; extraordinary communications respecting distant persons and places have been many times made with complete accuracy; and the spirits have represented themselves to the natural vision of some, and talked with them in an audible voice, the persons not knowing them to be spirits until they disappeared.

The astonishing progress of these wonders should awaken serious reflection on the part of every one. If these things continue to progress as hitherto, what a scene is there before us! It is evident that these things are but the beginning of the miracles with which the world is to be deceived. That all this is the work of demons, and not of the spirits of the dead, appears from several decisive facts, as follows:—

1. As to the dead, the Bible plainly testifies that they "know not anything" (Eccl. 9:5); that they are in the grave, where there is no work, nor device, nor knowledge, nor wisdom (verse 10); that they have laid down, and that they shall not awake, nor be raised out of their sleep, until the heavens be no more (Job 14:12); that they praise not the Lord (Isa. 38:18, 19; Ps. 115:17; 6:5); that in the day of death the thoughts perish (Ps. 146:2-4); and that if there is no resurrection, they which have fallen asleep in Christ have perished. 1 Cor. 15:18. To this we may add, that God has most solemnly forbidden necromancy, which is the pretended science of dealing with the dead. Deut. 18:11; Isa. 8:19. We may all see for a certainty that the dead cannot impart knowledge to us when they have none for themselves; and hence may understand that God warns us against seeking knowledge from that source, as we shall only expose ourselves to the delusion of the Devil.

2. The Bible clearly predicts that in the last days Satan is at work with all power, and signs, and lying wonders; that the spirits of devils are to work miracles; and that they will come in the guise of the spirits of the dead. We beg the reader to carefully compare 2 Thess. 2:9, 10 with Rev. 16:13-15 and Isa. 8:19-22. That the two-horned beast, which performs the miracles spoken of in Rev. 13, is the same as the false prophet from whose mouth one of the unclean spirits issues (chap. 16:13), we shall hereafter prove.

3. The third reason for regarding these as the spirits of devils is found in the fact that they most

openly contradict the authority of the Holy
Scriptures. They deny the resurrection of the
dead, the second advent of Christ, the Judgment,
and, indeed, all the leading doctrines of the Christian religion; they place the most profligate and
wicked men, like the infidel Paine, in the highest
heaven, and represent him as engaged in the same
work that he so faithfully adhered to while he
lived, viz., the overthrow of the authority of the
Bible; and, finally, they openly deny the inspiration of the word of God, and seek to substitute in
its place their own worthless fables.

The foregoing facts are, in short, the most important reasons that prove them to be these spirits of devils, and they can be appreciated by every
person who fears God and trembles at his word.
We have referred to the unclean spirits as the
agency by which the miracles of the two-horned
beast are to be performed. As proof that we are
correct in this, we refer to Rev. 16: 13, where one
of the three unclean spirits is represented as going
out of the mouth of the false prophet to perform
miracles. A comparison of Rev. 13: 11–17 with
19: 20, as we shall notice hereafter, proves that
the two-horned beast and the false prophet are
the same; hence it is certain that the unclean
spirits are the agency by which the two-horned
beast performs his miracles.

But these miracles are to be carried so far that
fire is to be brought down from heaven upon the
earth in the sight of men. In the days of Elijah,
the test between Jehovah and Baal was this very
thing: the god that could cause fire to come down
from heaven in the sight of the assembled multitude, was the true God. Satan was not then
able to perform this astonishing miracle. 1

Kings 18.   But this very act, by which the true
God was distinguished from the false, is now to
be performed by Satan himself.   This shows, as
we think, that this act of the two-horned beast
relates to the hour of temptation that shall come
upon all the world, to try them that dwell
upon the earth.   Rev. 3: 10, 11.   Who will be
prepared to resist such miracles as this?—None
but those who are especially kept by God.   The
multitude will inevitably be carried away by
them.   The truth of God, that shows all this to
be the work of the Devil, will then be the only
shield.   Those only who have kept the word of
God's patience will be kept in that time.   This
fearful hour of temptation, when Satan shall
work with all power and signs and lying wonders, is before us, and who will stand when it
shall come upon all the world?   "Watch ye,
therefore, and pray always, that ye may be accounted worthy to escape all these things that
shall come to pass, and to stand before the Son
of man."   Luke 21: 36.

CHAPTER VII.

THE WORK OF THE TWO-HORNED BEAST.

Influence of this Power upon the Nations—Its Deceptive Character—Identity of the Two-horned Beast with the False Prophet—The Dragon Voice of the Beast—The Image of the Beast—His Mark and the Number of his Name—The Worship of the Beast—The Final Contest.

No form of power ever arose in any past age combining the remarkable features which appear in our own government. It is of itself a wonder, a system of government which has not its like elsewhere. What is needed throughout the world to relieve its inhabitants of their oppression, but that Republicanism should remodel all their civil governments? The leaven of its principles has deeply diffused itself throughout the nations of the earth. In proof of this, witness the revolutions of 1848, which shook nearly all the thrones of Europe. And what is so well calculated to develop and maintain religious freedom as Protestantism? With the diffusion of these principles, how many are now confidently expecting a long period of prosperity and triumph for the church,—a period of emancipation to the poor enslaved nations of the earth,—the ushering in of the period when the nations shall learn war no more, and a universal spiritual kingdom shall be set up and fill the whole earth (Micah 4: 1–5); and those wonders which we have briefly noticed promise to mankind a better revelation than the Scriptures of truth afford us?

The people of God, indeed are looking forward to the time when the Lamb, who is King of kings and Lord of lords, shall reign in person over the whole earth. But with the mass this view has given place to the more congenial idea of a spiritual reign, and of temporal prosperity and triumph. This view holds out to men the prospect of peace and safety (1 Thess. 5), notwithstanding the evidence has been spread out before them that the hour of God's Judgment has come, and that no better state of things can ever exist till the curse shall be removed from the earth. The warning respecting the coming storm of wrath has been most faithfully given; but by the multitude it has been rejected, thus leaving them to the deceptions that are already coming upon the earth. They dream that the earth, with all its progress and all its improvements, is far too lovely and excellent for God to destroy. Peace and safety is the delusive dream in which men indulge while the wrath of God hangs over them.

We regard the two-horned beast, then, as the symbol of a civil and religious power, differing in many respects from those which have preceded it. It is in appearance the mildest form of power that ever existed; but it is, after having deceived the world with its wonders, to exhibit all the tyranny of the first beast. If the right of private judgment be allowed by the Protestant Church, why does she expel men from her communion for no greater crime than that of attempting to obey God in something wherein his word may not be in accordance with her creed? Read Charles Beecher's work, "The Bible a Sufficient Creed." Why are men, for no other crime than looking for Jesus Christ, expelled from the churches of those who profess to love his appearing?

To these and many other questions of a similar character, we can only answer, that the lamb is such only in pretension; he is dragon in character. His ostensible appearance is that of a lamb; but the power which he exercises is that of a dragon. The true kingdom of the Lamb, the King of kings, is not set up on the earth until the destruction of all the wicked powers that now bear rule. Then the Jubilee will end the bondage of the saints. God speed the right!

A further view of the two-horned beast may be obtained by comparing his history with that of the false prophet. The two-horned beast is represented as working miracles in the sight of the first beast. Rev. 13:14. The same is affirmed respecting the false prophet. Chap. 19:20. The nations of the earth are deceived by these miracles, and caused to worship the image of the first beast, and to receive his mark. The same work is ascribed to the false prophet. Still further, we may say that the Bible gives us the origin of the two-horned beast, but does not under that name give us his final destiny. The origin of the false prophet is not given under that name, but his destiny is clearly revealed. Rev. 19:20; 20:10. Inasmuch as their work is identical, and they act their part at the same time, we cannot doubt their identity. This is positive proof that the two-horned beast is, from the time of its rise, a power contemporary with the first beast, and not the first beast in another form. What power has ever risen in the past history of the world that could answer the description of this lamb-dragon, or false prophet? If Satan has been permitted to make use of paganism as an instrument of oppression and deception, and also of papacy, which is Christianity in a corrupt form, why may he not make use of Protestantism also, when it becomes corrupt, as, if possible, a more efficient means of deception than either of the former?

Has not the Protestant Church acted the part of the false prophet most effectually in promising to the world a thousand years of peace and prosperity before the day of wrath? She has prophesied this out of her own heart, for God has ever spoken the reverse. 2 Tim 3; Dan. 7; Matt. 13; 2 Thess. 2. The Protestant Churches as a body now proclaim this doctrine as expressing the great object for which they labor,—temporal prosperity and triumph in a world that has ever rejected Christ.

Mohammedanism is not this false prophet; for it is introduced in the prophecy under the symbol of locusts, and its power departed with the hour, day, month, and year of the second woe. Rev. 9. But the two-horned beast, or false prophet, acts as an accomplice of the papacy in Satan's great work of final deception, and unites in the great conflict against the King of kings. Rev. 19.

The work of deception prepares the way for the dragon voice of the beast. He says "to them that dwell on the earth, that they should make an image to the beast which had a wound by a sword, and did live." And thus it would seem that the history of this symbol is in part, at least, twice presented, each time ending with its oppressive acts, first, with its power represented by horns like a lamb, and subsequently exercising all the dragonic power of the first beast ; and, secondly, as a power working miracles to deceive the dwellers upon the earth ; and when this deception is accomplished, it is to cause them to unite in making an image that should have power to put every one to death who would not worship it. In noticing the prophetic history of the first beast, we called attention to the fact that the prediction respecting the time when all that dwell upon the earth whose names are not written in the book of life shall worship the beast, has never yet met its fulfillment ; and we would here express the conviction that this prophecy relates to the time when the two-horned beast is to speak as a dragon, and to exercise all the power of the first beast. In that hour of strong temptation, we may expect to see all the dwellers upon the earth united in the worship of the beast.

The beast was the papacy clothed with power to put to death the saints of God. Rev. 13 : 5–8 ; Dan. 7 : 23–26. An image to the beast, then, must be another ecclesiastical body clothed with power and authority to put the saints to death. This can refer to nothing else but the corrupt and fallen Protestant Church. If it be asked whence the beast receives this power, we can only answer that, by permission of God, the dragon, that old serpent, called the Devil and Satan, is without doubt the very being who communicates this power to the beast. The kingdoms of this world are claimed by him, and the right to give them to whom he will. Luke 4 : 5, 6. Should it be objected that the world is too much enlightened to submit to such deception, or to unite in such a work of persecution, we answer that the word of God gives us this prophecy in clear language ; and it is with reference to this scene of danger that the third angel utters his solemn warning. Look at the Jewish Church, and mark how soon after they had rejected the Messiah at his first coming, they put him to a cruel death, and also slew many of his apostles and saints. They said, indeed (Matt. 23), that had they lived in the days of their fathers, they would not have been partakers with them in the blood of the prophets ; but when their "hour and the power of darkness" came upon them, how completely did it show them to be under the power of Satan. Luke 22 : 53 ; John 7 : 30.

The rejection of the truth of God leaves men the captives of Satan, and the subjects of his deception. 2 Thess. 2 : 9–12. The greater the light which men reject, the greater the power of deception and of darkness which will come upon them. The advent message has been given in our own land, and by the mass rejected, and no greater, and indeed no other, light can ever be given to those who have turned away from that. The third angel gives us warning of the danger which is now before us. The warning precedes the danger, that we, by seasonable admonition, may make our escape.

Another religious power enforces the claims of the first beast and his image, and causeth the world to receive his mark. What is this mark of the beast ?—It is the mark of that beast to whom the image was made—the first beast. Rev. 19 : 20 ; 16 : 2. But it is enforced by the two-horned beast ; hence we understand it is an institution of the papacy, enforced by Protestantism. The beast and his image unite in this thing, in opposition to the saints, who are engaged in keeping the commandments of God. Have we an institution of the papal apostasy which the civil power supports, and to which the religious world pays homage ?—We have. It is found in a weekly sabbath, which the "man of sin" has placed in the stead of the Sabbath of the fourth commandment. If we turn to the law of God, we shall find that the fourth commandment alone points out Jehovah, the first three forbid the worship of false gods, and blasphemy, and the last six pertain wholly to our duty to our fellow-men. Not one of these nine commandments points out the true God. But the Sabbath commandment points out the true God as that being who in six days created heaven and earth, and rested upon the seventh. By the observance of the sanctified rest-day of the Creator, he is acknowledged as the true God, in distinction from every object upon which the eye can rest, in the heavens above or in the earth beneath. The being that created all these things is God. Such is the teaching of the fourth commandment.

But the Scriptures plainly predict that the man of sin should exalt himself above all that is called God, or that is worshiped, and should "THINK TO CHANGE TIMES AND LAWS." 2 Thess. 2 ; Dan. 7: 25. It is not said that he should be able to change them ; but he should think to do it ; or, as the Catholic version reads, "He shall think himself ABLE to change times and laws." They are not the times and laws of men which he thinks to change, for these he might be able to change, as other powers have done ; but it is an act of arrogance in which he does not succeed. The times and laws of God are doubtless intended. This apostasy began in the apostolic age (2 Thess. 2 : 7), and it has resulted in the perfect development of the man of sin, and of his blasphemous acts, among which we may name the change of the fourth commandment. No one can produce any other authority for changing the Sabbath than Romish traditions.

Listen to the following cutting reproof from a Romanist :—

"The word of God commandeth the seventh day to be the Sabbath of our Lord, and to be kept holy ; you [Protestants] without any precept of Scripture, change it to the first day of the week, only authorized by our traditions. Divers English Puritans oppose against this point, that the observation of the first day is proved out of the Scripture, where it is said the first day of the week.   Acts 20 : 7 ; 1 Cor. 16 : 2; Rev. 1 : 10.   Have they not spun a fair thread in quoting from these places ? If we should produce no better for purgatory and prayers for the dead, invocation of the saints, and the like, they might have good cause indeed to laugh us to scorn."*

Notwithstanding the fourth commandment in the plainest terms enjoins the observance of the sanctified rest-day of the Lord, almost all the world now wonders after the beast, and observe the pagan festival of Sunday, which the great apostasy has substituted for the holy Sabbath. By the observance of the Sabbath, men acknowledge the great Creator as their God ; but when they *understandingly* choose in its stead the sabbath of the man of sin, they acknowledge him as above all that is called God, or that is worshiped,

---

*See "History of the Sabbath," and "Who Changed the Sabbath ?" published at the *Review and Herald* Office.

and as able to change the times and laws of God. *There is no evading this point.* If we observe the Sabbath of the Lord, and that of the apostasy also, we only make the man of sin equal with God. But when we profane the Lord's Sabbath, and observe in its stead the Romish festival of Sunday, we acknowledge the papacy to be above God, and able to change his times and laws. We speak of those who have the light of truth and act contrary to it. *Those who have never yet understood that the observance of Sunday is a tradition of the fathers which makes void the fourth commandment, are not referred to. It is the bringing of this sabbath of the apostasy to the test that will constitute it the mark of that power that should think to change times and laws.* There is no other papal institution that directly sets aside one of the ten commandments, that the whole Protestant world observes. This mark is very conspicuous in the forehead or hand, and signifies not a literal mark, but a public profession, or act, that all may see or know.

The number of the name of the beast is also to be enforced as a test of submission to him. This name, which is said to be that of a man, is seen, without doubt, in the title of "Vicar of the Son of God," which the pope has caused to be inscribed upon his mitre. It is written in Latin, and the numeral letters employed make the sum of 666. The design of this test is to cause men to acknowledge the authority of the papacy.

The manner in which the Protestant Church would enforce the sabbath of the man of sin, had it the power, is well expressed by a distinguished clergyman.

Says Dr. Durbin. "I infer, therefore, that the

civil magistrate may not be called upon to enforce
the observance of the Sabbath, as required in the
spiritual kingdom of Christ; *but when Christianity becomes the moral and spiritual life of the
State,* the State is bound, through her magistrates,
to prevent the open violation of the holy Sabbath,
as a measure of self-preservation. She cannot,
without injuring her own vitality and incurring
the divine displeasure, be recreant to her duty in
this matter." *

It is proper that we should speak with careful-
ness of that which relates to the events of the future. That the scene described in the conclusion
of Rev. 13 pertains to the time of trouble before
us, such as never was, we have no doubt. It is
also evident that in the providence of God the
line of separation between the worshipers of the
beast and his image on the one hand, and those
who keep the commandments of God and the
faith of Jesus on the other, will be most distinct and visible. The third angel's proclamation will prepare the people of God for the coming
crisis; and the formation of the image and the reception of the mark will prepare all the various
classes of adherents to the beast, to receive the
vials of the wrath of God, the seven last plagues.
The image of the beast, as we have seen, is made
up of apostate religious bodies. The name of the
beast, as given in verse 1, is "Blasphemy." † The
mark will determine to which class each individual belongs. We have seen the cause of danger

---

* *Christian Advocate and Journal.*

† For extended remarks concerning the *image, mark,* and
number of the *name,* see the "Marvel of Nations."

fully laid open before us in Rev. 13. We now return to the voice of warning as presented in chap. 14: 9–11.

The warning of danger is a warning which refers directly to the scene of trouble described in Rev. 13: 11–18. This warning shows that that trouble is yet to come. Its fearful character may be learned from the thrilling and dreadful import of the angel's message. The Bible nowhere else depicts such dreadful wrath. On one side stands the decree of the beast, who is to exercise all the power of the first beast before him, that all who will not worship the image and receive his mark shall be put to death; on the other hand stands the solemn warning of the third angel. Here, then, is the strait before us. We can worship the beast and his image, and as the penalty, drink the wine of the wrath of God, or we can refuse, and peril our lives here, that we may obey God.

This message will draw a line between the worshipers of God and the worshipers of the beast and his image; for on either hand it reveals a dreadful penalty, and leaves no chance for half-way work. Those who disregard this warning will be found with the worshipers of the beast and his image, and will drink of the wine of the wrath of God. Those who heed this warning will obey God at the risk of their lives. The one class is designated by the mark of the beast, the other class is seen in the patience of the saints, keeping the commandments of God. That the law of God should thus be made a great testing truth to draw a line between the subjects of the fourth and fifth kingdoms, is an idea not unworthy of the God of the Bible. That the commandments of God are the great subject of controversy between the dragon and the remnant of the seed of the woman, is plain from Rev. 12:17. The issue of this struggle cannot be a matter of doubt; for, as in all past ages those who have had the ark of God and have kept his commandments have triumphed, even so will it be now.

What, then, is it to worship the beast? for this is a prominent part of the act against which the wrath of God without mixture of mercy is denounced, and, as we have seen, all the world are yet to unite in this act. It is worthy of notice that at the conclusion of this dreadful warning the saints are introduced as keeping the commandments of God and the faith of Jesus. Thus we may understand that the worship of the beast and his image, and the reception of his mark, is the opposite of keeping the commandments of God and the faith of Jesus. And we have seen that one of the commandments of God has been superseded by an institution of the Romish apostasy.

A remark by Prof. Bliss, bearing on this point, is worthy of lasting remembrance: "Whenever any civil or ecclesiastical enactment conflicts with the requisitions of Jehovah, that power is worshiped which is obeyed in preference to the other. 'Know ye not, that to whom ye yield yourselves servants to obey, his servants ye are to whom ye obey?' Rom. 6:16." *

We have already seen that the conflict is between the commandments of God and the requirements of the beast; and that a papal institution, which has usurped the place of one of the commandments of God, is yet to be made a test by

---

* "Bliss on the Apocalypse," p. 233.

the two-horned beast. It is not difficult, therefore, to see how men will be made to worship the beast; for whenever they obey the requirements of the beast in the place of the commandments of God, they worship the beast; for they acknowledge him as above the Most High. It is a remarkable fact that the pagan festival of Sunday, which the great apostasy has substituted for the Sabbath of the Bible, is now enforced by law in most of the States of the Union. A papal institution which directly contradicts the fourth commandment is thus enforced by a Protestant government!

But many of our State governments have already enacted that the Sabbath of the Bible (?) shall be kept on Sunday, and the judges have decided such laws to be constitutional! If the government has a right to nullify the fourth commandment, there is an end to the principle of religious liberty; for it has an equal right to nullify any or all of the others.

It may be proper that we should notice some of the most probable causes that will induce the two-horned beast to create the image, and to require the reception of the mark:—

1. The first which we should name is the work of the spirits in performing miracles, etc. It is certain that this agency, as we have already seen, is to deceive the dwellers upon the earth, and to cause them to make the image which all must worship on pain of death. We may rest assured that this extraordinary development of Satanic power has been reserved by him to act an important part in preparing men for the seven last plagues. If our public men become mediums (and some of them are such already), and our

citizens become believers in this new system of divinity, our government is hopelessly in the hands of the Devil. Such a result may be neither improbable nor distant.

2. A second cause, and one, too, which should not be lightly passed over, is this : The preaching of the commandments of God and the faith of Jesus. This is the cause of the conflict between the dragon and the last fragment of the church. We shall hereafter show that the commandments of God, as distinguished from the faith or testimony of Jesus, mean the ten commandments. The fourth of these commandments the dragon has attempted to change. It is because the saints are keeping all the commandments of God that the dragon makes war upon them. This prophecy (Rev. 12 : 17) doubtless refers to the scene described in the conclusion of Rev. 13. Mr. Miller remarks respecting this prophecy: "I am therefore constrained to believe this battle of the dragon's last power will be in America; and if so, it must be mainly in these United States."*

It is because the commandments of God will be vindicated, and the unscriptural character of the Sunday-sabbath exposed, that the two-horned beast will require all to receive the mark. The lack of *scriptural* argument has been the chief cause why men have resorted to the argument of fire and fagot to convince dissenters.

---

* "Lectures," p. 213.

CHAPTER VIII.

THE PENALTY THREATENED BY THE THIRD ANGEL.

A Fearful Penalty—The Seven Last Plagues—The Third Woe—
The Lake of Fire—Limited Duration of Final Conflagration
—New Heavens and New Earth—Recompense of the Right-
eous—Annihilation of the Wicked.

THE fearful penalty connected with the warning of the third angel now claims our attention.
It consists of two things: 1. The wine of the
wrath of God, poured out without mixture into
the cup of his indignation; 2. The torment with
fire and brimstone in the presence of the holy
angels and of the Lamb. Let us carefully consider each in order. What is the wine of the
wrath of God? The next chapter clearly explains
this point: "And I saw another sign in heaven,
great and marvelous, seven angels having the seven
last plagues; for in them is filled up the wrath
of God." "And one of the four beasts gave
unto the seven angels seven golden vials, full of
the wrath of God, who liveth forever and ever."
Verses 1, 7. It follows, therefore, that the wine
of the wrath of God is the seven last plagues.
This fact will be further apparent as we proceed
to show that these plagues are future, and that
they do pertain to the future we think can be established beyond controversy.

1. The wrath of God, as threatened by the
third angel, is poured out in the seven last
plagues; for the first plague is inflicted on the
very class that the third angel threatens. Compare Rev. 14: 9, 10; 16:1, 2. The fact proves
that the plagues must be future when the Third

Angel's Message is given; and it also proves the identity of the wrath of God without mixture with the seven last plagues.

2. We have shown that the plagues and the wrath of God without mixture are the same. And wrath without mixture must be wrath with nothing else; that is, wrath without mercy. God has not yet visited the earth with unmixed wrath; nor can he while our great High Priest ministers in the heavenly Sanctuary, and stays the wrath of God by his intercession for sinful men. When the plagues are poured out, mercy has given place to vengeance.

3. Hence it is that the seven angels are represented as receiving the vials of the wrath of God —the seven last plagues—after the opening of the Temple of God in heaven. If we turn to Rev. 11:15-19, we shall find that the opening of the Temple in heaven is an event that transpires under the sounding of the seventh angel. And that account concludes with a brief statement of the events of the seventh vial, or last plague. Now if we turn to chap. 15:5-8 and 16:1-21, we shall read an expanded view of the facts stated in chap. 11:15-19, and we shall find that the two accounts conclude in the same manner, viz., with the events of the last plague. These scriptures show that the seven angels do not receive the vials of the wrath of God to pour out upon the earth until the Temple in heaven is opened. That Temple is opened under the voice of the seventh angel. The third woe is by reason of the voice of the seventh angel. Rev. 8:13; 9:12; 11:14. The seven plagues are poured out under the sounding of that angel; hence the plagues are future, and constitute the third woe.

The foregoing reasons establish the fact that the plagues are future. We see no reason why they will not be similar in character to those poured out on Egypt, while their consequences will be far more terrific and dreadful. We will now briefly compare the account of these plagues with other scriptures calculated to shed light upon the subject. The first vial is thus presented : "And the first went and poured out his vial upon the earth ; and there fell a noisome and grievous sore upon the men which had the mark of the beast, and upon them which worshiped his image." Rev. 16 : 2.

This may be best understood by referring to Ex. 9 : 8–11 : "And the Lord said unto Moses and unto Aaron, Take to you handfuls of ashes of the furnace, and let Moses sprinkle it toward the heaven in the sight of Pharaoh. And it shall become small dust in all the land of Egypt, and shall be a boil breaking forth with blains upon man and upon beast, throughout all the land of Egypt. And they took ashes of the furnace and stood before Pharaoh ; and Moses sprinkled it up toward heaven ; and it became a boil breaking forth with blains upon man and beast. And the magicians could not stand before Moses because of the boil ; for the boil was upon the magicians, and upon all the Egyptians."

Why will not the antetype be as real and literal ? The wine of the wrath of God unmixed with mercy must be far more dreadful than the judgment inflicted on Egypt. The second and third vials are thus presented : "And the second angel poured out his vial upon the sea ; and it became as the blood of a dead man ; and every living soul died in the sea. And the third angel poured out his vial upon the rivers and fountains of waters ; and they became blood.   And I heard the angel of the waters say, Thou art righteous, O Lord, which art, and wast, and shalt be, because thou hast judged thus : for they have shed the blood of saints and prophets, and thou hast given them blood to drink ; for they are worthy. And I heard another out of the altar say, Even so, Lord God Almighty, true and righteous are thy judgments."   Rev. 16 : 3–7.

As an illustration of these plagues, read Ex. 7: 17–21 : "Thus saith the Lord, In this thou shalt know that I am the Lord ; behold, I will smite with the rod that is in mine hand upon the waters which are in the river, and they shall be turned to blood.   And the fish that is in the river shall die, and the river shall stink ; and the Egyptians shall loathe to drink of the water of the river. And the Lord spake unto Moses, Say unto Aaron, Take thy rod, and stretch out thine hand upon the waters of Egypt, upon their streams, upon their rivers, and upon their ponds, and upon all their pools of water, that they may become blood; and that there may be blood throughout all the land of Egypt, both in vessels of wood and in vessels of stone.   And Moses and Aaron did so, as the Lord commanded ; and he lifted up the rod, and smote the waters that were in the river, in the sight of Pharaoh, and in the sight of his servants ; and all the waters that were in the river were turned to blood.   And the fish that was in the river died ; and the river stank, and the Egyptians could not drink of the water of the river : and there was blood throughout the land of Egypt."

The third vial is a retribution for the blood of

the saints. As the blood of all the righteous that had been slain upon the earth came upon that generation which rejected Christ at his first advent (Matt. 23 : 34–36), so also may it be now. It should be remembered that these fearful judgments are inflicted in consequence of the acts described in the conclusion of Rev. 13. "And the fourth angel poured out his vial upon the sun ; and power was given unto him to scorch men with fire. And men were scorched with great heat, and blasphemed the name of God, which hath power over these plagues ; and they repented not to give him glory. And the fifth angel poured out his vial upon the seat of the beast; and his kingdom was full of darkness ; and they gnawed their tongues for pain, and blasphemed the God of heaven, because of their pains and their sores, and repented not of their deeds." Rev. 16 : 8–11.

The scorching of the fire in the midst of their trouble will be terrible in the extreme. Ex. 10 : 21–23 will illustrate the fifth vial : "And the Lord said unto Moses, Stretch out thine hand toward heaven, that there may be darkness over the land of Egypt, even darkness which may be felt. And Moses stretched forth his hand toward heaven ; and there was a thick darkness in all the land of Egypt three days ; they saw not one another, neither rose any from his place for three days ; but all the children of Israel had light in their dwellings."

On this subject, Litch remarks : "What a terrible scene ! with all their grievous sores, blood to drink—stagnant blood—and putrid fish filling the waters, scorched with burning heat ; and then, to crown the whole, the kingdom of Antichrist is to be full of darkness. Oh, what a picture of woe ! Reader, make haste to escape it! 'Watch ye, therefore, and pray always, that ye may be accounted worthy to escape all these things that shall come to pass, and stand before the Son of man.'"

"And the sixth angel poured out his vial upon the great river Euphrates ; and the water thereof was dried up, that the way of the kings of the East might be prepared. And I saw three unclean spirits like frogs come out of the mouth of the dragon, and out of the mouth of the beast, and out of the mouth of the false prophet. For they are the spirits of devils, working miracles, which go forth unto the kings of the earth and of the whole world, to gather them to the battle of that great day of God Almighty. Behold, I come as a thief. Blessed is he that watcheth, and keepeth his garments, lest he walk naked, and they see his shame. And he gathered them together into a place called in the Hebrew tongue, Armageddon." Rev. 16 : 12–16.

The effect of the sixth vial will be, first, to prepare the way for the kings of the East to come up to the great battle ; and, secondly, to send forth the spirits of devils to deceive, by miracles, the kings of the whole earth, and their armies, and to gather them.

The battle of the great day of God Almighty is very fully described in Jer. 25 :—

"For thus saith the Lord God of Israel unto me, Take the wine cup of this fury at my hand, and cause all the nations, to whom I send thee, to drink it. And they shall drink, and be moved, and be mad, because of the sword that I will send among them. Then I took the cup at the Lord's hand, and made all the nations to drink, unto whom the Lord had sent me." "And all the kings of the North, far and near, one with another, and all the kingdoms of the world, which are upon the face of the earth; and the king of Sheshach shall drink after them." "Therefore, prophesy thou against them all these words, and say unto them, The Lord shall roar from on high, and utter his voice from his holy habitation; he shall mightily roar upon his habitation; he shall give a shout as they that tread the grapes, against all the inhabitants of the earth. A noise shall come even to the ends of the earth; for the Lord hath a controversy with the nations; he will plead with all flesh; he will give them that are wicked to the sword, saith the Lord. Thus saith the Lord of hosts, Behold, evil shall go forth from nation to nation, and a great whirlwind shall be raised up from the coasts of the earth. And the slain of the Lord shall be at that day from one end of the earth even unto the other end of the earth; they shall not be lamented, neither gathered, nor buried; they shall be dung upon the ground." Verses 15-17, 26, 30-33.

The coming of Christ as a thief (see Matt. 24: 42-44) does not take place until after the sixth vial is poured out. The gathering of the nations to the great battle, which is accomplished by the spirits, is brought to view in many scriptures. Joel 3: 1, 2, 9-16; Zeph. 3: 8; Rev. 19: 19-21.

The present development of the spirits of devils in our land, we do not regard as anything but their preparatory work; for there is always a period in which Providence is preparing those agents which are to fulfill prophecy; but the fulfillment of prophecy begins at the point where the agents

are prepared to act the predicted part. Thus
Rome, though it constituted the fourth empire,
was founded when Babylon, the first empire, was
in the hight of its glory. But when Greece, the
third empire, had fulfilled its part, Rome was
prepared to act the part assigned it in prophecy.
It is thus that we understand the work of the
spirits. Under the sixth plague, the spirits will
be prepared to act the part predicted in verse 13.

"And the seventh angel poured out his vial
into the air; and there came a great voice out of
the Temple of heaven, from the throne, saying,
It is done. And there were voices, and thunders,
and lightnings; and there was a great earthquake,
such as was not since men were upon the earth,
so mighty an earthquake, and so great. And the
great city was divided into three parts, and the
cities of the nations fell; and great Babylon came
in remembrance before God, to give unto her the
cup of the wine of the fierceness of his wrath.
And every island fled away, and the mountains
were not found. And there fell upon men a
great hail out of heaven, every stone about the
weight of a talent; and men blasphemed God because of the plague of the hail; for the plague
thereof was exceeding great." Verses 17–21.

The voice from the temple may be illustrated
by the following texts: "The Lord, also, shall
roar out of Zion, and utter his voice from Jerusalem; and the heavens and the earth shall shake;
but the Lord will be the hope of his people, and
the strength of the children of Israel." Joel 3:16.
"Therefore, prophesy thou against them all
these words, and say unto them, The Lord shall
roar from on high, and utter his voice from his
holy habitation; he shall mightily roar upon his

habitation; he shall give a shout as they that tread the grapes, against all the inhabitants of the earth. A noise shall come even to the ends of the earth; for the Lord hath a controversy with the nations; he will plead with all flesh; he will give them that are wicked to the sword, saith the Lord." Jer. 25: 30, 31.

The great earthquake may also be found spoken of in other scriptures: "The earth is utterly broken down, the earth is clean dissolved, the earth is moved exceedingly. The earth shall reel to and fro like a drunkard, and shall be removed like a cottage; and the transgression thereof shall be heavy upon it; and it shall fall, and not rise again." Isa. 24: 19, 20. "And the heaven departed as a scroll when it is rolled together; and every mountain and island were moved out of their places." Rev. 6: 14; 11: 19.

The great hail out of heaven is well illustrated by the following scriptures: "And the Lord said unto Moses, Stretch forth thine hand toward heaven, that there may be hail in all the land of Egypt, upon man, and upon beast, and upon every herb of the field, throughout the land of Egypt. And Moses stretched forth his rod toward heaven; and the Lord sent thunder and hail, and the fire ran along upon the ground; and the Lord rained hail upon the land of Egypt. So there was hail, and fire mingled with the hail, very grievous, such as there was none like it in all the land of Egypt since it became a natian. And the hail smote throughout all the land of Egypt all that was in the field, both man and beast; and the hail smote every herb of the field, and brake every tree of the field." Ex. 9: 22–25. "Hast thou entered into the treasures of the snow, or hast thou seen the treasures of the hail, which I have reserved against the time of trouble, against the day of battle and war?" Job 38 : 22, 23. "Judgment, also, will I lay to the line, and righteousness to the plummet; and the hail shall sweep away the refuge of lies, and the waters shall overflow the hiding-place." Isa. 28 : 17.

Such is a brief view of the dread realities of the seven last plagues,—the third woe! How fearful will be the events of that woe! May God count us worthy to escape the things coming on the earth, and to stand before the Son of man.

The seven last plagues are poured out on the living wicked; but the second part of the penalty affixed to the warning of the third angel, is not inflicted until the end of the thousand years, when all the wicked are raised and suffer together. This part of the penalty we will now consider.

"He shall be tormented with fire and brimstone in the presence of the holy angels, and in the presence of the Lamb; and the smoke of their torment ascendeth up forever and ever," etc. The final perdition of ungodly men in the lake of fire is without doubt the subject of these awful words. That we may rightly understand this text, we call attention to several important facts:—

1. The punishment of the wicked will be inflicted upon them on this earth; for the final conflagration of our globe is to constitute the lake of fire in which they are to be rewarded, each according to his works. "Behold, the righteous shall be recompensed in the earth; much more the wicked and the sinner." Prov. 11 : 31. "But the heavens and the earth, which are now, by the same word are kept in store, reserved unto fire

against the day of Judgment and perdition of ungodly men." 2 Peter 3:7. "But the fearful and unbelieving, and the abominable, and murderers, and whoremongers, and sorcerers, and idolaters, and all liars, shall have their part in the lake which burneth with fire and brimstone; which is the second death." Rev. 21:8. "For behold, the day cometh that shall burn as an oven; and all the proud, yea, and all that do wickedly, shall be stubble; and the day that cometh shall burn them up, said the Lord of hosts, that it shall leave them neither root nor branch." Mal. 4:1. "And when the thousand years are expired, Satan shall be loosed out of his prison, and shall go out to deceive the nations which are in the four quarters of the earth, Gog and Magog, to gather them together to battle; the number of whom is as the sand of the sea. And they went up on the breadth of the earth, and compassed the camp of the saints about, and the beloved city; and fire came down from God out of heaven and devoured them." Rev. 20:7–9.

2. The prophet Isaiah (chap. 34) describes the final conflagration of our globe in language which is a complete parallel to that of the third angel in describing the punishment of the wicked. Those who contend that Isaiah refers only to ancient Idumea, must admit that the period of time described in this strong language must finally come to an end. And those who admit that Isaiah, in the language we are about to quote, refers to the conflagration of our earth, will find in what follows, ample proof that that scene will finally close.

"For it is the day of the Lord's vengeance, and the year of recompenses for the controversy of

Zion. And the streams thereof shall be turned into pitch, and the dust thereof into brimstone, and the land thereof shall become burning pitch. It shall not be quenched night nor day; the smoke thereof shall go up forever; from generation to generation it shall lie waste; none shall pass through it forever and ever." Isa. 34:8–10.

3. But this terrific scene of final conflagration is not to last throughout unlimited duration. For the earth having been burned, and all its elements melted, new heavens and a new earth are to follow, as the present earth succeeded to that which was destroyed by water. And in the earth thus made new the righteous are to be recompensed. "But the day of the Lord will come as a thief in the night; in the which the heavens shall pass away with a great noise, and the elements shall melt with fervent heat, the earth also; and the works that are therein shall be burned up. Seeing then that all these things shall be dissolved, what manner of persons ought ye to be in all holy conversation and godliness; looking for and hasting unto the coming of the day of God, wherein the heavens being on fire shall be dissolved, and the elements shall melt with fervent heat? Nevertheless, we, according to his promise, look for new heavens and a new earth, wherein dwelleth righteousness." 2 Pet. 3:10–13. "And I saw a new heaven and a new earth; for the first heaven and the first earth were passed away; and there was no more sea." Rev. 21:1.

4. Thus, however dreadful and long-continued the punishment of the wicked will be (for each is to be punished according to his deserts), that punishment will finally result in the utter de-

struction of all transgressors. All the wicked
will God destroy. Ps. 145:20. They shall die
the second death. Rev. 21:8; Rom. 6:23; Eze.
18:4, 20. They shall perish, being consumed
into smoke. Ps. 37:10, 20, 38. They shall be
punished with everlasting destruction, being
burned up in unquenchable fire. 2 Thess. 1:9;
Matt. 3:12. And thus, having been consumed,
root and branch, they shall be as though they
had not been. Mal. 4:1. Obadiah 16.

CHAPTER IX.

CHRONOLOGY OF THE THIRD ANGEL.

The Patience of the Saints—The Commandments of God—
Opening of the Temple in Heaven—The Wrath of God
without Mixture—The Faith of Jesus—Practical Duties—
The Time of Trouble—The Triumph of the Saints—Conclusion.

WE will now briefly refer to several important
facts that prove that the present is the period in
which the warning of the third angel is to be
given. We have proved that the proclamations
of the first and second angels belong to that generation that is to witness the final overthrow of
all earthly powers, and the sublime scenes of the
second advent; and that the present is that generation that shall witness these fearful events.
We have also shown that the two former proclamations have already been made, and consequently the warning of the third angel is the great
theme which should now arrest the attention of
every mind. The chronology of this message
seems to be distinctly marked by the fact that it

is given in the period of the "patience of the saints," which follows the proclamation of the two former messages. "Here is the patience of the saints; here are they that keep the commandments of God, and the faith of Jesus." Verse 12. And this period of the saints' patience is marked by a most important fact, viz., the keeping of the commandments of God and the faith of Jesus. We wish to call attention to several points:—

1. We have shown that the First Angel's Message refers to the solemn proclamation of the immediate second advent; consequently the period of patience here brought to view must be the same as that which in many scriptures is located immediately preceding the second advent. A few texts must suffice as examples: "Cast not away therefore your confidence, which hath great recompense of reward. For ye have need of patience, that after ye have done the will of God, ye might receive the promise. For yet a little while, and he that shall come will come, and will not tarry. Now the just shall live by faith; but if any man draw back, my soul shall have no pleasure in him. But we are not of them who draw back unto perdition, but of them that believe to the saving of the soul." Heb. 10:35-39.

"Be patient, therefore, brethren, unto the coming of the Lord. Behold, the husbandman waiteth for the precious fruit of the earth, and hath long patience for it, until he receive the early and latter rain. Be ye also patient; stablish your hearts; for the coming of the Lord draweth nigh. Grudge not one against another, brethren, lest ye be condemned; behold, the Judge standeth before the door. Take, my brethren, the prophets, who have spoken in the name of the Lord, for an example of suffering affliction and of patience." James 5 : 7–10.

"Because thou hast kept the word of my patience, I also will keep thee from the hour of temptation, which shall come upon all the world, to try them that dwell upon the earth. Behold, I come quickly ; hold that fast which thou hast, that no man take thy crown." Rev. 3 : 10, 11.

"And it shall be said in that day, Lo, this is our God ; we have waited for him, and he will save us ; this is the Lord ; we have waited for him, we will be glad and rejoice in his salvation." Isa. 25 : 9.

2. The period of the saints' patience, here brought to view, is distinguished by the fact that they are keeping the commandments of God, and the faith of Jesus. It should be distinctly noticed that the commandments here brought to view are not the commandments of Christ. There may be a certain sense in which all the precepts of the Saviour may be called the commandments of God ; that is, if viewed as proceeding from the sovereign authority of the Father ; but when the commandments of God are spoken of in *distinction* from the testimony or faith of Jesus, there is but one thing to which reference can be made ; viz., the commandments which God gave in person,—the ten commandments. See John 15 : 10 : "If ye keep my commandments, ye shall abide in my love ; even as I have kept my Father's commandments, and abide in his love." And thus we find the law of God, which he proclaimed in person, referred to in the New Testament as the "commandments of God," or as the "commandments."

" And He said unto him, Why callest thou me good ? there is none good but one, that is God ; but if thou wilt enter into life, keep the commandments.   He saith unto him, Which?   Jesus said, Thou shalt do no murder, Thou shalt not commit adultery, Thou shalt not steal, Thou shalt not bear false witness, Honor thy father and thy mother, and Thou shalt love thy neighbor as thyself."   Matt. 19 : 17–19.

" And they returned and prepared spices and ointments ; and rested the Sabbath-day according to the commandment."   Luke 23 : 56.

" Think not that I am come to destroy the law, or the prophets : I am not come to destroy, but to fulfill.   For verily I say unto you, Till heaven and earth pass, one jot or one tittle shall in no wise pass from the law, till all be fulfilled.   Whosoever therefore shall break one of these least commandments, and shall teach men so, he shall be called the least in the kingdom of heaven ; but whosoever shall do and teach them, the same shall be called great in the kingdom of heaven." Matt. 5 : 17–19.

" Honor thy father and thy mother ; which is the first commandment with promise ; that it may be well with thee, and thou mayest live long on the earth."   Eph. 6 : 2, 3.

" But he answered and said unto them, Why do ye also transgress the commandment of God by your tradition ? For God commanded, saying, Honor thy father and mother ; and he that curseth father or mother, let him die the death. But ye say, Whosoever shall say to his father or his mother, It is a gift by whatsoever thou mightest be profited by me ; and honor not his father or his mother, he shall be free. Thus have

ye made the commandment of God of none effect
by your tradition." Matt. 15 : 3-6.

"What shall we say then? Is the law sin?
God forbid. Nay, I had not known sin but by
the law ; for I had not known lust, except the
law had said, Thou shalt not covet. But sin,
taking occasion by the commandment, wrought
in me all manner of concupiscence. For without
the law, sin was dead. For I was alive without
the law once ; but when the commandment came,
sin revived, and I died. And the commandment,
which was ordained to life, I found to be unto
death. For sin, taking occasion by the commandment, deceived me, and by it slew me.
Wherefore, the law is holy ; and the commandment holy, and just, and good. Was then that
which is good made death unto me ? God forbid.
But sin, that it might appear sin, working death
in me by that which is good ; that sin by the
commandment might become exceeding sinful.
For we know that the law is spiritual ; but I am
carnal, sold under sin." Rom. 7 : 7-14.

It is a fact beyond dispute that the fourth
commandment, some ages since, was changed
from the rest-day of the Lord to the pagan festival of Sunday. This change was made in express contradiction of the Holy Scriptures, which
everywhere recognize the seventh day as the only
weekly Sabbath of the Lord. It was ·accom-
plished by the great apostasy, which Daniel predicted should "think to change times and laws."
This power is essentially the same as the beast
which was to be worshiped by all the world.
And it is a fact of deep interest that this commandment, which has been so long trodden down,
is now being vindicated, and the people of God

are striving to keep it with the other nine.
Thanks be to God that he is preparing the remnant for their final conflict with the dragon,
and for admittance through the gates into the
holy city. Rev. 12 : 17 ; 22 : 14. The vindica-
tion of the fourth commandment in opposition to
the Sabbath of the apostasy, and the preaching
of all the commandments of God, is a striking
testimony that the present is the period of the
saints' patience, and of the warning of the third
angel.

3. The opening of the holiest of all in the Temple in heaven, by which the ark is seen, is an
event that takes place under the sounding of the
seventh angel. And as the ministration of our
great High Priest is changed to that apartment
at the termination of the 2300 days,* we understand that the opening of the Temple is marked
by the termination of that period, as presented
by the proclamation of the first angel. The entrance of our High Priest into the most holy place
to minister before the ark of God, calls the attention of the church to the commandments of God
contained within that ark. The commandments
of God have been shining out from the heavenly
Sanctuary since that time.

The period between our Lord's entrance into
the holiest of all to cleanse the Sanctuary (Heb. 9:
23) and complete his great work of ministration,
and the close of that period as marked by the
seven angels' coming out of the Temple to pour
out the vials of the wrath of God upon the earth
(Rev. 15:5, 6), we understand to be the period of
the saints' patience. It is the days of the voice

---

* See works on the Sanctuary.

of the seventh angel in which the mystery of God is being finished; that is, the period when human probation is brought to a close. Besides the fact of the termination of the 2300 days, which marks the opening of the Temple in heaven, the anger of the nations is an important testimony that we are now in the days of the voice of the seventh angel. Rev. 11:18. The present time is, therefore, the proper period for the last message of mercy to perishing men; and it is marked by the actual presentation of that voice of warning, and of the commandments of God, and the faith of Jesus.

4. Another important fact that determines the chronology of the third angel is that the seven last plagues are poured out upon those who reject his warning, the first plague being inflicted upon the very class which the third angel threatens. The seven last plagues are the wine of the wrath of God, poured out without mixture into the cup of his indignation. We have already seen that they are not inflicted until the work of mercy for man is accomplished. The third angel warns us respecting this outpouring of the exterminating wrath of God, and consequently gives the latest message of mercy. The mystery of God, or work of salvation for sinful men, (Eph. 3) is finished in the days of the voice of the seventh angel, when he begins to sound (Rev. 10); and as the third angel has the last warning of mercy before the vials of God's wrath are poured out, it follows that it must be given in the days when the seventh angel begins to sound. It is likewise evident that the conclusion of the work of our great High Priest in the heavenly Sanctuary must also take place in the days when the seventh angel

begins to sound; for it is then that the mystery
of God is finished.

The reason why the third woe, or seven last
plagues, does not commence at once when the
seventh angel begins to sound, is the fact that a
period of days is occupied in finishing the mystery of God. In this period the warning of the
third angel is given, that every one who has an
ear to hear may escape the vials of the wrath of
God; and in this period, also, the Saviour com-
pletes his work in the Sanctuary in heaven.
This being accomplished, the vials of the wrath of
God are poured out upon the defenseless heads of
the wicked. We think, therefore, that the evidence is conclusive that the present is the time
for the warning of the third angel. A false fulfillment of prophecy cannot occur at the time
when the true should be expected. It is certain
that one of the commandments of God has long
been trodden down by the beast, and that in this
thing almost the whole world has wondered after
the beast. This commandment, as well as all the
others, is now being vindicated, that the remnant
may be prepared for their final conflict with the
dragon. May God interest the hearts of all his
people in this work.

We have already briefly spoken of the commandments of God; a few words should be devoted to the faith of Jesus. This term is used in
distinction from the commandments of God.
What, therefore, shall we understand by the
"faith of Jesus"? We think that it cannot refer to a particular degree or kind of faith which
the Saviour exercised in the performance of his
miracles; for it appears that he wrought these by
the power which he had already received from
his Father. Matt. 8:2, 3; Mark 1:40, 41; Luke

5: 23, 24. The world itself was made by him.
John 1. He had ample power, therefore, to perform every miracle which he wrought. There is
but one other thing to which this term can refer;
viz., the precepts and doctrines of our Lord, as
recorded in the New Testament. Thus, "the
faith of the gospel" (Phil. 1: 27) must refer to
the precepts and doctrines of the gospel. "The
faith" to which a multitude of the priests were
obedient (Acts 6: 7), which was resisted by Ely-
mas, the sorcerer (Acts 13: 8), which was committed to the apostles for the obedience of all nations (Rom. 1: 5), which Paul testifies that he had
kept (2 Tim. 4: 7), and which is to be earnestly
maintained, as once delivered to the saints (Jude
3), must refer, we think, to the precepts and doctrines of the everlasting gospel. That the faith
of Jesus is used in this sense in Rev. 2: 13, we
think cannot be denied. "Thou holdest fast my
name," says Jesus, "and hast not denied my
faith." That this is the sense in which it is used
in Rev. 14: 12, is further evident from the fact
that it is spoken of as being kept in the same
manner that the commandments of God are kept.

It remains that we notice a few of the most
important practical duties that devolve upon us
at the present time:—

1. First of all we would mention holy living.
God has committed to our trust the most precious
truths, and he holds us responsible for the light
with which we are intrusted. "Let your light
so shine before men, that they may see your good
works, and glorify your Father which is in
heaven." Matt. 5: 16. The sanctifying effect of
the truth must be witnessed in us by others, if
we would do them good. Especially must we
watch unto prayer. Watchfulness and prayer are

mighty weapons with which to resist the Devil. Their importance may be seen from the following scriptures:—

"Be sober, be vigilant; because your adversary, the Devil, as a roaring lion, walketh about, seeking whom he may devour; whom resist, steadfast in the faith, knowing that the same afflictions are accomplished in your brethren that are in the world." 1 Pet. 5:8, 9. "Praying always with all prayer and supplication in the Spirit, and watching thereunto with all perseverance and supplication for all saints." Eph. 6:18. "And I say unto you, Ask, and it shall be given you; seek, and ye shall find; knock, and it shall be opened unto you. For every one that asketh, receiveth; and he that seeketh, findeth; and to him that knocketh it shall be opened." Luke 11:9, 10. "If any man offend not in word, the same is a perfect man, and able also to bridle the whole body." James 3:2. "But the end of all things is at hand: be ye therefore sober, and watch unto prayer." 1 Pet. 4:7. "But I say unto you, That every idle word that men shall speak, they shall give account thereof in the day of Judgment; for by thy words thou shalt be justified, and by thy words thou shalt be condemned." Matt. 12: 36, 37.

2. Growth in grace. It is greatly to be feared that the importance of this is too much lost sight of. If we would be final overcomers and stand upon Mount Zion, we must be daily overcoming the great foe of our souls. The long-suffering of God is meant for our salvation. Let us most faithfully improve the gracious opportunity now granted us to perfect holiness in the fear of the Lord.

"But grow in grace, and in the knowledge of our Lord and Saviour Jesus Christ." 2 Pet. 3: 18. "Follow peace with all men, and holiness, without which no man shall see the Lord." Heb. 12: 14. "But as He which hath called you is holy, so be ye holy in all manner of conversation; because it is written, Be ye holy; for I am holy." 1 Pet. 1:15, 16.

3. The duty of searching the Scriptures. This is solemnly enjoined by our Lord. John 5:39. Without this, we cannot obey the precept of Peter: "Be ready always to give an answer to every man that asketh you a reason of the hope that is in you, with meekness and fear." 1 Pet. 3:15. The sword of the Spirit, the word of God, is an important part of the armor which God has prepared for us. Eph. 6. It is certain that events before us are such that every person will be tested. If the truth of God is understood, appreciated, and loved by us, we must examine the Scriptures for ourselves. If it is not loved, the time is not distant when we shall be sifted out. Everything is before us to deceive and lead astray. The spirits of devils are about to perform the most extraordinary miracles. They will do this, professing to be the spirits of our departed friends. Hence the great importance of a thorough knowledge of the Bible doctrine of the sleep of the dead. The Lord would not have us ignorant concerning them which are asleep.

4. The duty of sacrificing to sustain the cause of God. There is no plainer duty in the Scriptures. Ourselves, our time, our means, all that we have, all that we are, belong to God alone. Those who go out to preach the word of God are called upon to make the greatest sacrifice. All

are not called to do this; but those who are not, if they love Christ and the truth, will gladly sustain those who are thus thrust out. Let not the cause of truth suffer for the means to sustain it. Read Rom. 12:1; 2 Cor. 8; Luke 12:33, 34; 1 John 2:15; Matt. 6:19-34.

5. The duty of waiting and watching for our Lord's return. Let this ever be our position, and let all our words and acts be in accordance with our profession, that the end of all things is at hand. "Watch ye, therefore; for ye know not when the Master of the house cometh, at even, or at midnight, or at the cock-crowing, or in the morning; lest coming suddenly he find you sleeping. And what I say unto you I say unto all, Watch." Mark 13 : 35-37. "But ye, brethren, are not in darkness, that that day should overtake you as a thief. Ye are all the children of light, and the children of the day: we are not of the night, nor of darkness. Therefore let us not sleep, as do others ; but let us watch and be sober." 1 Thess. 5:4-6. "And unto them that look for him shall he appear the second time without sin unto salvation." Heb. 9:28. "Let your loins be girded about, and your lights burning; and ye yourselves like unto men that wait for their Lord, when he shall return from the wedding; that when he cometh and knocketh, they may open unto him immediately. Blessed are those servants, whom the Lord when he cometh shall find watching; verily I say unto you, that he shall gird himself, and make them to sit down to meat, and will come forth and serve them." Luke 12:35-37.

6. Finally, let us indeed be Bible Christians. Let the commandments of God and the faith of

Jesus be the continual rule of our lives, and the governing principle of our conduct. May the great Head of the church help us all to perfect holiness in the fear of the Lord.

CONCLUSION.

WE have now briefly and imperfectly surveyed this most important subject. Sufficient evidence has been adduced, we think, to satisfy the honest inquirer that we occupy one of the most solemn and interesting periods in the history of the church. The first and second proclamations of Rev. 14 are in the past, and the warning voice of the third angel is now addressed to us; the fearful scenes of Rev. 13:13–17 are about to open upon us; and last of all, the seven last plagues are soon to be poured out upon those who, regarding the decree of the beast more than the warning of the third angel, shall be found worshiping the beast and his image, and possessing his mark. Who among us will be able to meet the fearful test between the warning of the third angel and the decree of the beast? Let him that thinketh he standeth, take heed lest he fall.

The situation of the church when the decree goes forth that all shall worship the image of the beast on pain of death, will be precisely that of the three Hebrew worthies whom Nebuchadnezzar commanded to worship the golden image. Read carefully Dan. 3. God saved them by direct interposition. He has promised thus to interpose for his people; but it will not be until the time of trouble, such as never was, has fully opened upon the world. With this fearful prospect of the coming storm before us, we may well appreciate the words which follow the warning of the third angel. "And I heard a voice from Heaven, saying unto me, Write, Blessed are the dead which die in the Lord from henceforth. Yea, saith the Spirit, that they may rest from their labors, and their works do follow them." Rev. 14:13. The following scriptures will show us why those are pronounced blessed who now fall asleep in Christ, and will also show the situation of the saints at the time when God delivers them:—

"And at that time shall Michael stand up, the great Prince which standeth for the children of thy people; and there shall be a time of trouble, such as never was since there was a nation even to that same time; and at that time thy people shall be delivered, every one that shall be found written in the book." Dan. 12:1. "Alas! for that day is great, so that none is like it: it is even the time of Jacob's trouble; but he shall be saved out of it." Jer. 30:7. "Oh that thou wouldest hide me in the grave, that thou wouldest keep me secret, until thy wrath be past, that thou wouldest appoint me a set time, and remember me!" Job 14:13. "When I heard, my belly trembled; my lips quivered at the voice; rottenness entered into my bones, and I trembled in myself, that I might rest in the day of trouble: when he cometh up unto the people, he will invade them with his troops." Hab. 3:16. "And the Lord said, Hear what the unjust judge saith. And shall not God avenge his own elect, which cry day and night unto him, though he bear long with them? I tell you that he will avenge them speedily. Nevertheless when the Son of man cometh, shall he find faith on the earth?" Luke 18: 6–8.

Finally, we see the unclean spirits preparing for the great battle. We see the preparation for the law which shall compel all men to observe Sunday. We see the papal power awakening to declare itself infallible, and to claim anew the power to rule over the kingdoms of the earth. We hear the voice of alarm of the third angel, and we already see many thousands in response to his warning turning to the observance of God's commandments. These things are striking signs of the great day of God now just before us.

The conflict with the beast and his image is inevitable; but the issue of this conflict is not a matter of doubt. God will interpose to save his people. Though the last act of Satan be to unite all the wicked of the earth in the worship of the beast, and to attempt the utter extermination of the saints, yet God has said that the saints shall triumph!

"And I saw as it were a sea of glass mingled with fire; and them that had gotten the victory over the beast, and over his image, and over his mark, and over the number of his name, stand on the sea of glass, having the harps of God. And they sing the song of Moses the servant of God and the song of the Lamb, saying, Great and marvelous are thy works, Lord God Almighty; just and true are thy ways, thou King of saints." Rev. 15: 2, 3.

Glorious indeed will be the triumph of the saints! Reader, may it be your lot to join in singing that song of victory upon the sea of glass.

We'd love to send you a free catalog of titles we publish
or even to hear your thoughts, reactions, criticisms,
about things you did or did not like about this
or any other book we publish.

Just write or call us at:

TEACH Services, Inc.

800/367-1998

www.tsibooks.com